So Near, So Far
Ryan Preciado —
Manuel Sandoval

So Near, So Far
Ryan Preciado —
Manuel Sandoval

Palm Springs Art Museum

Contents

Rita Gonzalez
& Ryan Preciado

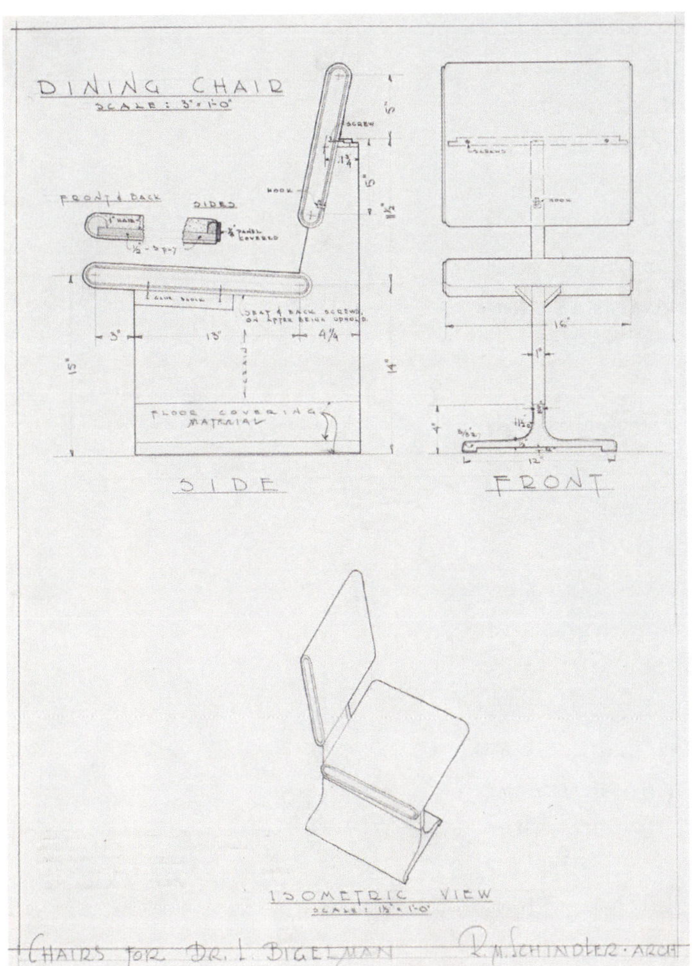

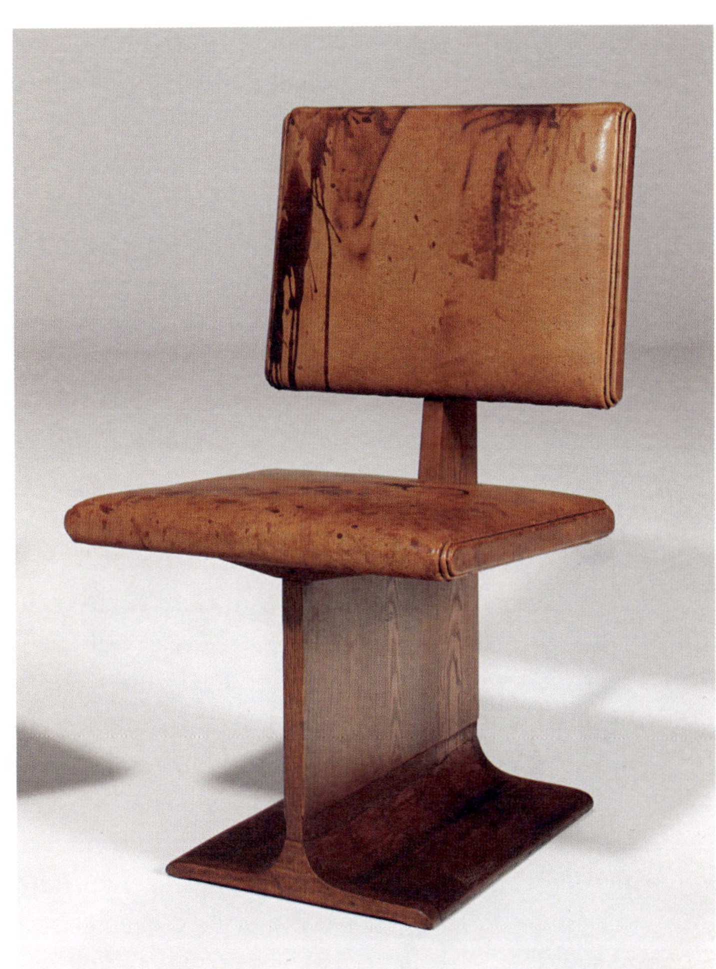

Left:
R. M. Schindler, technical drawing for
dining chair, 1944

Right:
R. M. Schindler dining chair, 1946

Rita Gonzalez: How did you find out about Manuel Sandoval? When did you realize that you wanted to do a project that intersects with your interest in him?

Ryan Preciado: It was early into the pandemic. This project became my way of dealing with isolation. My friend Andrew Romano, who owns the [Ralph G.] Walker House designed by R. M. Schindler, called to ask if I would be interested in replicating a dining set that had originally been made for that house. In the information Andrew sent me about the dining set I came across the name Manuel Sandoval for the first time. I gathered that Sandoval was Frank Lloyd Wright's saving grace. He was Wright's carpenter, and the architect would recommend Sandoval to colleagues. Schindler needed a dining set design once before the Walker House and there was only one guy who was to be trusted. Because I had never heard Sandoval's name, I was interested in doing what little research I could to find out more about him—most of which

Andrew had already dug up. I found out that Sandoval started as an apprentice in the Taliesin Fellowship, founded by Wright and his wife Olgivanna Lloyd Wright, with an interest in architecture, but was not let out of the woodshop once Wright found out how good he was. Wright referred to Manuel at times as "that" or "my Mexican" . . . He was from Nicaragua. Discovering Sandoval felt like finding a piece of history that had been invisible, and I wanted to play a small part in making it visible. We believe the Walker House dining chairs and table took Sandoval seven months—it took me a year to replicate them.

RG: So did part of what you learned about Sandoval come through actually learning how he made work? Did you get a sense of where Wright's designs stopped and Sandoval's hand came in?

RP: I started to look at all of the furniture in buildings designed by Wright as Manuel's. I had a dream in the middle of all of this that Wright was learning about Mayan culture through Sandoval and that's what inspired him to design the Hollyhock House and continue with Mayan Revival. In the dream, Sandoval and Wright were collaborating on all of the Mayan Revival houses. Later, I was talking with a friend and found myself sharing events from the dream as if they were real. I guess it was wishful thinking on my part. After the dream, I found some original pieces that Sandoval made before he went to Taliesin—a Mayan-style carved cabinet and desk. They are inscribed "M. Sandoval." I'm trying to help write a history that's been erased.

RG: I wanted to say that the subtext of this project is Sandoval, but actually you are centering his work—it's not below the surface. Did you find echoes in your own experience working for other artists and designers?

RP: I can't say that I've been as valuable as Sandoval was to Wright and Schindler, but I have done my share of work on projects that had someone else's name on them. Being an assistant or an apprentice can be a really thankless job. It's always been clear to me that the difference between who does manual labor and who gets to be credited for design is so marked by class and race, but working on this project brought this idea of lost or invisibilized labor to a different level for me. It gave me the perspective to pay attention. I've been trying to pay attention actively ever since.

RG: One thing that really intrigued me as we prepared for this conversation was your story about finding smudged blueprints of one of Sandoval's dining chairs for the Walker House. Trying to replicate them, you had to interpolate and make design decisions even though information was missing in the materials that you had access to. You mentioned having an almost clairvoyant dialogue

Top:
Ryan Preciado, chair from Walker House dining set, 2020

Bottom:
Ralph G. Walker House interior, 1936

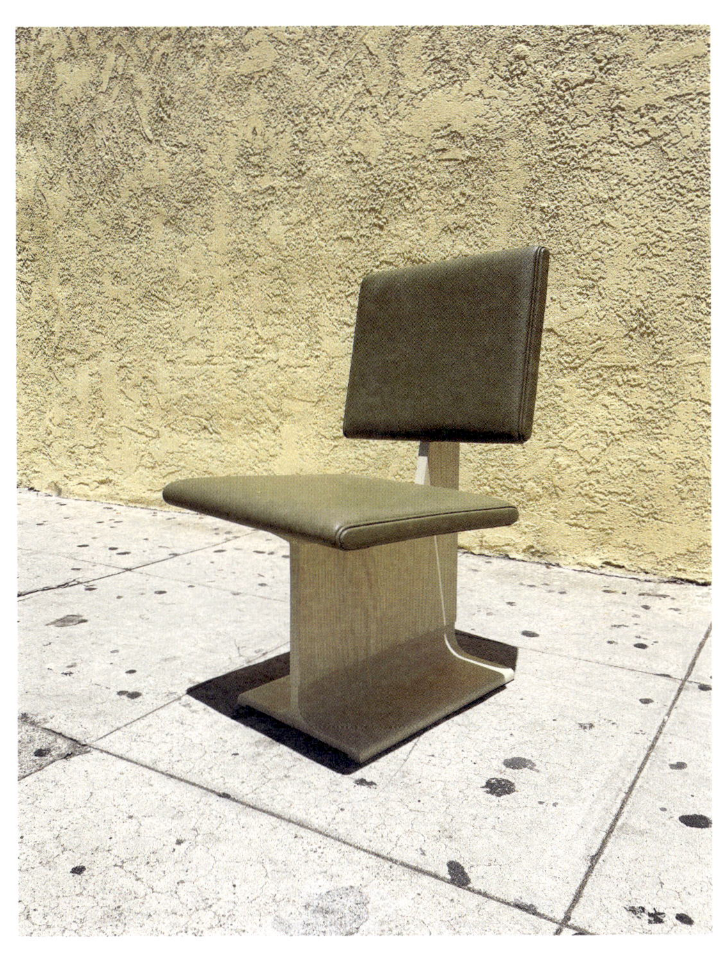

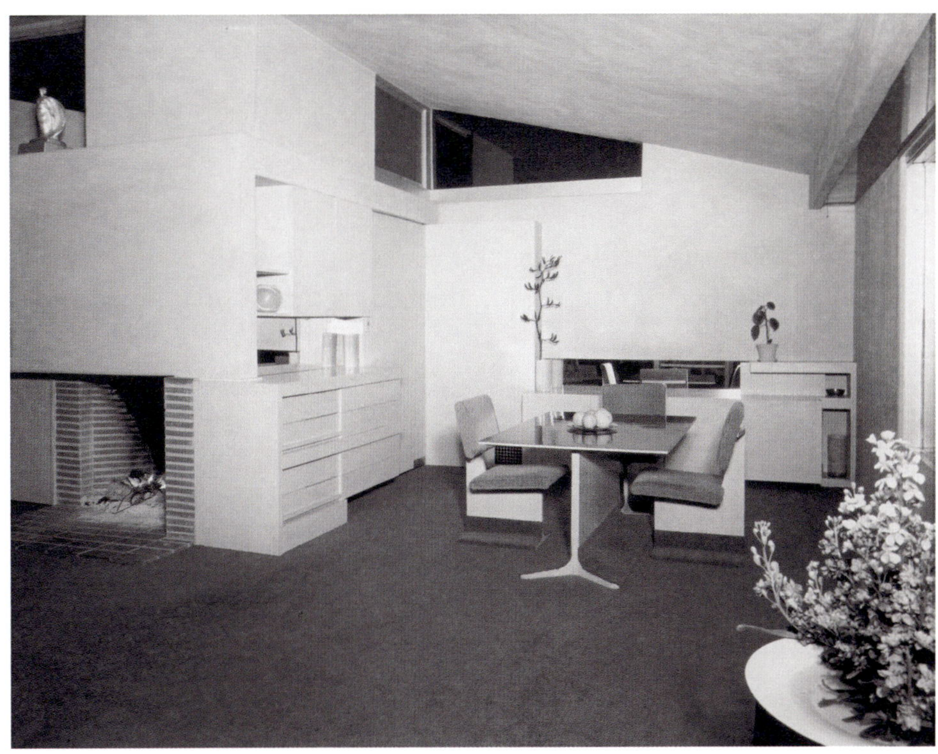

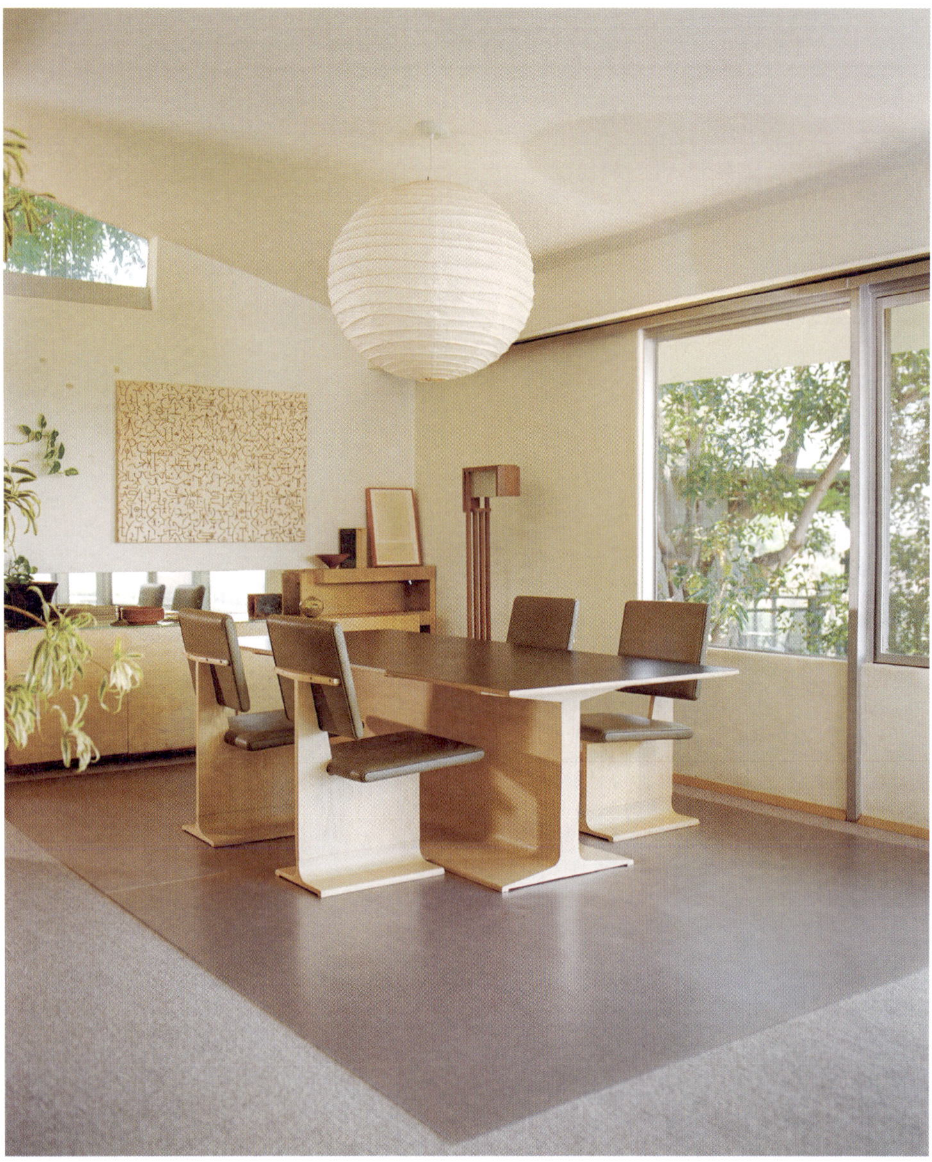

with Sandoval. Is this imagined conversation with design history something you have thought about in the past in relation to how you work?

RP: It just seemed like the natural thing to do in such an isolated time. I was alone at home and alone at the woodshop every day . . . it became normal to talk out loud to his spirit. It probably started out of frustration—not knowing how he did something and asking for advice. Trying to trace Sandoval's thoughts, I made a few works, like *Toro table* (2023) and a sideboard cabinet, after I started this project. In some way it felt like I was trying to impress a father figure. I remember wondering if he would like *Toro table* and what his version would have looked like. That was the first time I noticed how much he was influencing me, because I was working

Ryan Preciado, dining set, 2020. Interior view, Ralph G. Walker House, Los Angeles so directly in relation to someone else's work. I was metaphorically tracing someone else's hands. I absorb things pretty easily and was genuinely interested in the make of the Walker table. At first, modeling works after his wasn't a conscious decision and it happened at random times, but in the case of the *Toro table* there was some residual Sandoval. But now, on a more emotional level, I move through what I do while considering how Sandoval and others did not have the chance to show their own work. I am thinking about how fortunate I am and it's been a humbling experience. It feels like a life lesson.

RG: Could we go into a bit of detail about how your work interacts with Sandoval's in the exhibition?

RP: The majority of the exhibition consists of pieces I have based off of Sandoval's work, such as the stools he made for the V. C. Morris Gift Shop, along with archival materials and correspondence. We are showing the dining set that started all of this research. I made a box based on a story Robert [Kett] and I found online: Wright gave Sandoval a pencil and Sandoval made a velvet-lined box for it. He admired him so much. There is an original chair by Sandoval that I replicated. The conversation between my work and his is obvious when the objects are in the same room.

RG: Are you interested in people losing track of where his work ends and your work begins?

RP: I like that Sandoval's work stands out. I am interested in the fact that when people see his work they think of Wright, but like I said earlier, maybe now Sandoval will come into their head. I would like for his work and mine to be in conversation, because after working on this project, how could it not be? I'm just trying to fill the space so we can bring him back.

*Conversations
Across Time*
Robert J. Kett

1   For more on the contemporary restoration of the Ralph G. Walker House, see Andrew Romano, *The Walker House, RM Schindler* (Barcelona: Apartmento, 2018).

In 2020, Ryan Preciado began a conversation across time with the life and work of carpenter Manuel Sandoval. Asked to recreate furniture for the dining room of the Walker House, a Silverlake home designed by architect Rudolph M. Schindler, Preciado undertook a kind of forensics on a set of chairs made by Sandoval in the 1940s to understand how to achieve the deeply technical design.[1] Along the way, he compiled a list of questions for Sandoval—about his craft, his life, and how he navigated a crucial chapter in American architectural history.

We know that Sandoval was born in Nicaragua in 1898. (He is inaccurately described as Ecuadoran, Honduran, Mexican, or Spanish in correspondence and published accounts.) He learned to work in cabinetry from his father and immigrated to the United States sometime around 1917. Living in Chicago in the early 1930s, he applied to join Frank Lloyd Wright's Taliesin Fellowship in Wisconsin. Soon, Sandoval was involved in building Taliesin itself, models for Wright's studio, as well as furniture and interiors for some of the architect's major projects. After moving to California, he collaborated with other Wright apprentices who had also come west.

But the silences in Sandoval's story are of as much interest as the facts. His creative labor lay at the heart of projects credited to some of the most prominent architects in the United States, yet his name goes largely unmentioned. His own archive—a growing collection of correspondence, oral histories, and footnotes from historical accounts—is one that has to be assembled at the margins of others'.

Nothing could be more familiar to architectural historians than the work of Wright and his apprentices. However, the erasure of Sandoval's labor and celebration of the "genius" of the architects with whom he collaborated forces us to confront the limitations of accepted histories. Sandoval's experience of this period challenges traditional accounts centered on individuals like Wright. It reminds us that

THE TALIESIN FELLOWSHIP   SPRING GREEN   WISCONSIN

APPLICATION FOR FELLOWSHIP

NAME AND ADDRESS   MANUEL SANDOVAL   1118 North La Salle St. Chicago, Ill.

AGE 33   WEIGHT 145   HEIGHT 5'9"   PARENTS LIVING AND WHERE   Both dead in Nicaragua

RELIGIOUS AFFILIATION OF PARENTS   Catholic church

WHAT EDUCATION   Instituto Nacional de Rivas Nic.

PREVIOUS OCCUPATION   Cabinet making

PREDILECTION FOR WHAT PARTICULAR ART EXPRESSION · BUILDING   0

REMARKS   MUSIC

PAINTING

SCULPTURE

CRAFTS

THREE REFERENCES   Waldo B Stone, Chicago

Ramon Shiva   "

Robert P Schweikher   "

Manuel Sandoval, Taliesin Fellowship application, 1932

architecture results from the creative and bodily labors of many and that racism has often obscured these contributions.[2] Though Wright is famous for embracing (and appropriating) the *styles* of "Others" from Japan to Mesoamerica, acknowledging Sandoval's role in realizing these visions calls attention to the politics of race and labor in the making of twentieth-century architecture.[3]

This book and the exhibition at the Palm Springs Art Museum that inspired it borrow their title from a 1963 recording by Miles Davis. *So Near, So Far* was part of Preciado's recurring soundtrack in the studio as he worked to reconstruct Sandoval's carpentry in 2020, when the isolation of the COVID-19 pandemic prompted his dialogues with Sandoval—as a carpenter but also as a kind of ghost haunting architecture's archive. The track's title speaks to what we—myself, Preciado, and the archivists and others who helped our search—experienced while working through research and making: moments of connection despite the distance of time but also the frustrations of silence. It may never be possible to tell Sandoval's entire story. One of our hopes is that this project surfaces more fragments of an archive still being built from pieces.

This essay outlines chapters in Sandoval's life and career that informed Preciado's new work on view in *So Near, So Far.* Spanning works inspired by his own Chumash and Mexican American family, the techniques of the auto body shop where his works are painted,

2 Recently, historians have paid new attention to what Huda Tayob and Suzanne Hall describe as the connection of "space-making and race-making" in architecture. Understanding the place of race within the built landscape and architecture's own ways of working requires "writing race back into our understanding of modern architecture," in the words of the editors of *Race and Modern Architecture.* As they note, "race can be read as much within the canon as outside of it," by revisiting the familiar to understand what and whom it centers and excludes. See Tayob and Hall, *Race, space and architecture: towards an open-access curriculum* (London: London School of Economics and Political Science, 2019); Irene Chang, Charles L. Davis II, and Mabel O. Wilson, *Race and Modern Architecture: A Critical History from the Enlightenment to the Present* (Pittsburgh, PA: University of Pittsburgh Press, 2020), 4–10.

3 See, for example, Jesse Lerner, *The Maya of Modernism* (Albuquerque, NM: University of New Mexico Press, 2011); Jesse Lerner, "*Ch'u Mayaa* and the Appropriation of the Past," *21: Inquiries into Art, History, and the Visual – Beiträge zur Kunstgeschichte und visuellen Kultur* 4, vol. 2 (2023): 245–58.

WESTERN UNION

PATRONS ARE REQUESTED TO FAVOR THE COMPANY BY CRITICISM AND SUGGESTION CONCERNING ITS SERVICE 1204

CLASS OF SERVICE

This is a full-rate Telegram or Cablegram unless its deferred character is indicated by a suitable sign above or preceding the address.

NEWCOMB CARLTON, PRESIDENT J. C. WILLEVER, FIRST VICE-PRESIDENT

SIGNS
DL = Day Letter
NM = Night Message
NL = Night Letter
LCO = Deferred Cable
NLT = Cable Night Letter
WLT = Week-End Letter

The filing time as shown in the date line on full-rate telegrams and day letters, and the time of receipt at destination as shown on all messages, is STANDARD TIME.

Received at SPRING GREEN, WIS

AU M 47 NL

NC CHICAGO ILL SEPT 20 1932

FRANK LLOYD WRIGHT,

TALIESIN, SPRINGGREEN WIS.

EAGER TO JOIN COLONY AM EXPERT CARPENTER AS BILL LITTLE WILL TESTIFY

HAVE STUDIED ARCHITECTURE AT HOME READ YOUR INSPIRING AUTOBIOGRAPHY

AND HEARD CHICAGO LECTURES AM VERY MUCH IN EARNEST AGE THIRTY FIVE

LET ME COME PLEASE WRITE OR WIRE COLLECT ELEVEN EIGHTEEN NORTH

LASALLE STREET CHICAGO .

MANUEL J SANDOVAL.   842 PM

TELEGRAMS MAY BE TELEPHONED TO WESTERN UNION FROM ANY PRIVATE OR PAY-STATION TELEPHONE

Manuel Sandoval, telegram to Frank Lloyd Wright, September 20, 1932

4   Sandoval, telegram to Wright, September 20, 1932. The Frank Lloyd Wright Foundation Archives, Avery Architectural and Fine Arts Library, Columbia University, New York, Fiche ID: S024A07.

5   For more on Wright's personal life and its impact on his professional practice, see Meryle Secrest, *Frank Lloyd Wright: A Biography* (Chicago: University of Chicago Press, 1998).

6   For more on the model of communal pedagogy at Taliesin's founding and the precedents that informed it, see Edgar Tafel, *Apprentice to Genius: Years with Frank Lloyd Wright* (New York: McGraw-Hill, 1979), 136–37.

7   For more on Wright's conceptions of truth and unity, nature and society, and the intellectual genealogies that inform them, see William Cronon, "Inconstant Unity: The Passion of Frank Lloyd Wright," in *Frank Lloyd Wright: Architect*, eds. Terence Riley and Peter Reed (New York: The Museum of Modern Art, 1994), 8–31.

or the contents of his local hardware store, Preciado's projects have always paid a kind of reverence to the everyday, acknowledging forgotten moments of life, labor, and identity. He has brought the same perspective to sculptures that revisit historical designs by the likes of Mario Botta, Carlo Mollino, and Aldo Rossi, approaching them less as icons than as objects to be lived with and subsequently remade from new perspective. This mode of creative attention is at work in the furniture, objects, and reliefs Preciado has created for this exhibition. The designs he reimagines may have begun with the sketches of Wright and Schindler, but Preciado's work asks us to consider the labor and lives that have been left out of design history as we know it.

"EAGER TO JOIN COLONY"
Spring Green, Wisconsin

In September of 1932, Sandoval sent a telegram from Chicago to Spring Green, Wisconsin: "EAGER TO JOIN COLONY AM EXPERT CARPENTER . . . HAVE STUDIED ARCHITECTURE AT HOME." The message goes on to describe Sandoval's fascination with Wright, noting that he attended the architect's lectures in Chicago and was inspired by his autobiography. Wright's scribbled reply says that Taliesin "can use good carpenters."[4] He tells Sandoval to come immediately and that arrangements would be made for him to join the architect's new fellowship.

Founded that same year, the Taliesin Fellowship was tied to a place—a stretch of the Wisconsin River Valley settled by Wright's Welsh maternal family that the architect had reinvented as his own home, farm, and studio. Much like the Unitarian religious community founded there by his relatives, Taliesin represented a way of learning, working, and living. Grounded in a model of apprenticeship and "learning by doing," the fellowship was in part a pragmatic response to a period of deep uncertainty in Wright's career in the wake of personal scandal and the Great Depression.[5] Conceived in dialogue with his third wife Olgivanna, the fellowship combined the work of Wright's studio, the education and labor of fee-paying apprentices, and the running of Taliesin itself, including design and construction but also farming and cooking.[6] Perhaps more than any of his other work, Taliesin spoke to Wright's understanding of architecture as *Gesamtkunstwerk*—a total vision that knit together building, interiors, and furniture, but also a set of social ties and daily rhythms, a reflection of his vision of architecture as a pathway to realizing deeper truths.[7]

As a founding member of the fellowship, Sandoval worked extensively on carpentry and furniture for Taliesin. He made benches and chairs for the playhouse where fellows hosted film screenings to

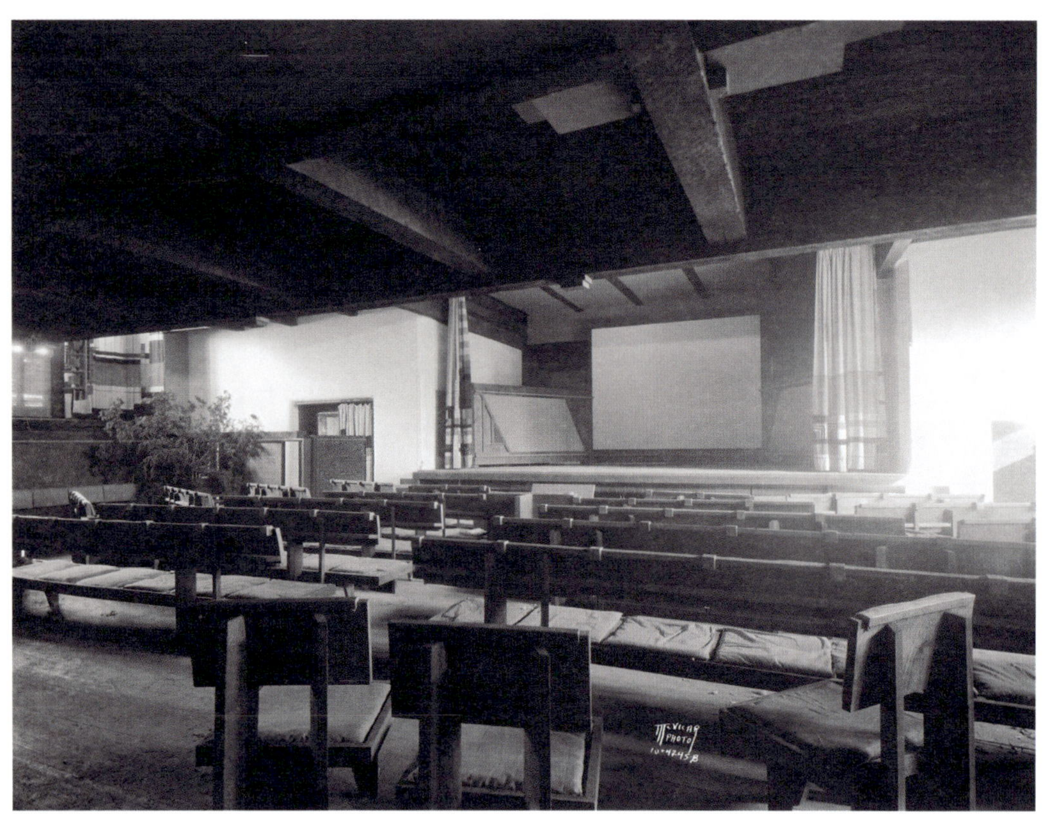

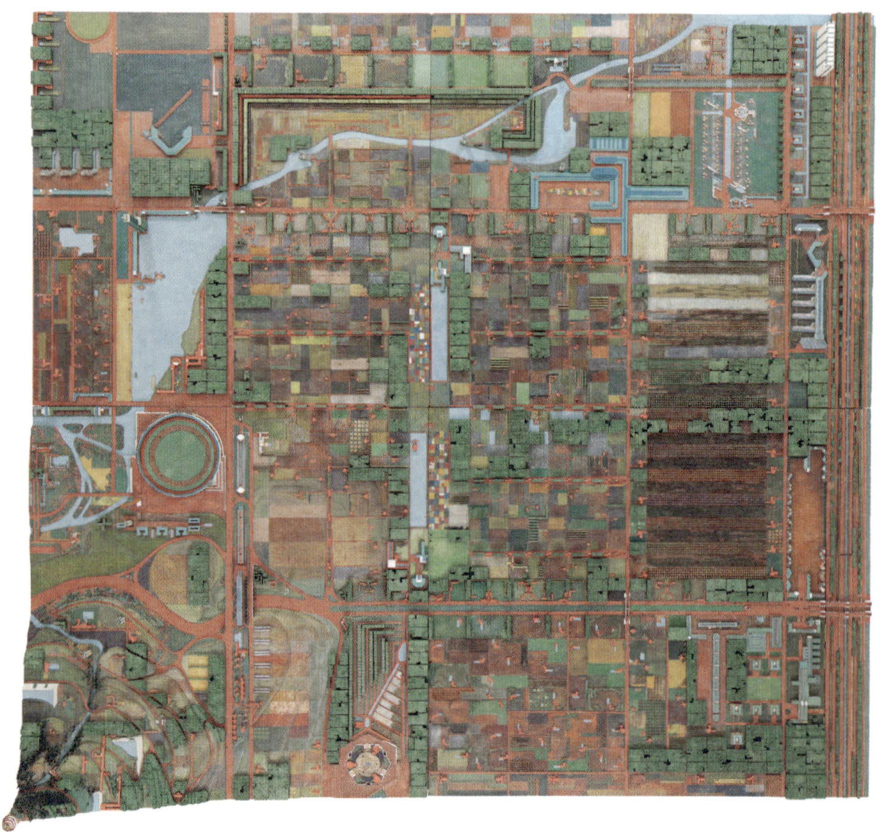

8 Margaret Allen, "At Taliesin: Enchanted Castle," April 6, 1934. Repr. in Randolph C. Henning, ed., *"At Taliesin": Newspaper Columns by Frank Lloyd Wright and the Taliesin Fellowship 1934–1937* (Carbondale, IL: Southern Illinois University Press, 1992), 34–35.

9 Tafel, *Apprentice to Genius*, 85–86.

10 Pedro E. Guerrero, *Pedro E. Guerrero: A Photographer's Journey* (New York: Princeton University Press, 2007), 20.

11 Bridget Bartal, "(Mis)fitting Taliesin: The Women of Frank Lloyd Wright's Taliesin Fellowship." Masters thesis (Bard Graduate Center, 2022), 13. Sandoval himself offered some of the only real design education at Taliesin to one of the fellowship's female members, Elizabeth Bauer Mock. He taught her "to construct her own version of a Morris chair" during a routine characterized more by everyday chores like ditch digging on the farm. See Wendy Lesser, "The Importance of the Personal," *Places Journal* (September 2022): https://placesjournal.org/article/elizabeth-bauer-mock/.

12 Cronon, "Inconstant Unity," 9.

13 Ibid., 17.

Top:
Playhouse, Taliesin, Spring Green, Wisconsin, 1933

Bottom:
Frank Lloyd Wright, model for Broadacre City, 1934–35

raise funds from the public, and he contributed to studio projects like Wright's model for his never-realized vision of Broadacre City, a suburban utopia centered on the automobile. Sandoval also traveled with the fellowship to spend their first winter in Arizona, in anticipation of Wright's eventual construction of Taliesin West there.

We can only guess at the reality of Sandoval's personal experience of Taliesin, a place of remarkable intimacy and intensity. In an essay on life there, fellow Margaret Allen described it as a "magic circle into which all who step believing are suddenly able to see with a clarity of vision undimmed by disillusionment and insincerity."[8]

However, Sandoval's place in this "magic circle" was likely an ambivalent one, inflected by the racism of the time. Allen's reflection includes an anecdote about Sandoval—described as "our master craftsman, a Spaniard and deeply imbued with the superstitious beliefs of his race"—mistaking the shadow of a runaway goat in his window for an apparition of the devil. During an unexpected detour through Canada on a road trip with Wright, Sandoval was detained by United States border officials.[9] These tensions between belonging and marginalization were shared by others who experienced Taliesin through the mark of difference. Pedro E. Guerrero, a Mexican-American photographer who later joined the fellowship at Taliesin West, described a similar experience in his own career: "No matter how much I achieved, I always felt the need to explain just who I was and why I belonged."[10] In her study of the women of Taliesin and their own struggles there, Bridget Bartal notes that "race [also] played an important role in misfitting at Taliesin."[11]

Compounding the racism experienced by fellows like Sandoval were the wider politics of labor at Taliesin. While the fellowship was advertised as a novel form of architectural training through practice, in reality the everyday lives of the fellows were usually occupied less with their own learning than the labor of realizing Wright's projects. As the environmental historian William Cronon describes, Wright's domineering vision of architecture imposed limitations on his students: "Although he constantly lectured them about the need for artistic independence and the paramount goal of developing their own individuality, in practice he demanded conformity, consistently refusing them the space to articulate any artistic vision at odds with the master's."[12] While many fellows' reflections on Taliesin are fond, they also speak to a prevailing sense of exploitation.

This was especially true for Sandoval. Though Sandoval joined the fellowship with the hope of studying architecture, Wright's initial excitement at Sandoval's carpentry skills was telling. As Cronon argues, the architect believed that "the decorative arts existed to serve architecture."[13] Sandoval's ability seems to have become a kind of burden. The fact that he became essential in fabricating Wright's designs left him marginalized within hierarchies of labor that centered on the drafting room. The architect's biographer recounts that Sandoval "had come to study architecture with the great man, but instead of being instructed, he felt he was kept doing fine cabinetry for Wright, work for which he was being highly paid in the outside world . . . Wright taught nothing in the accepted sense."[14]

These limits to the learning offered at Taliesin, along with the loss of better paying opportunities elsewhere, informed Sandoval's decision to leave the fellowship and return to Chicago in 1935. However, his experience in Wisconsin would continue to shape his life. As Guerrero reflected about a meeting with Wright after his own departure from the fellowship, "When I left that day, it was with the understanding that I would be on call . . . whenever he needed me."[15]

THE APPRENTICE LABORS
Pittsburgh, Pennsylvania

After leaving Taliesin, Sandoval returned to Chicago to live with his wife and reestablish his carpentry business. (Wright's preference that the fellows remained unmarried may also explain Sandoval's departure.) However, in April 1936, just months after Sandoval left Wisconsin, Wright turned to him to help realize one of a series of new commissions in Pittsburgh.

In 1934, Edgar Kaufmann Jr., the son of a Pittsburgh department store owner, joined the Taliesin Fellowship after studying in Europe and discovering Wright's architecture. As Christopher Wilk points out, Wright was "obviously aware of the Kaufmann family's wealth" when Kaufmann Jr. came to Taliesin and "as an architect eager to build, sent off to the elder Kauffman a portfolio of his work."[16] Wright's strategy was effective. Edgar J. Kaufmann Sr. was committed to the value of progressive design for his business and a dedicated supporter of Pittsburgh's urban development.[17] During mutual visits to Taliesin and Pittsburgh, Wright and Kaufmann Sr. discussed a trio of architectural commissions, including a renovation of Kaufmann's office at the department store, a proposal for a new planetarium in Pittsburgh, and the construction of a house for the Kaufmann family.

This latter project resulted in what may be Wright's best known work: Fallingwater (1934–37), a house perched on a waterfall on the Bear Run river about seventy miles outside of Pittsburgh. The renovation of Kaufmann's tenth-floor corner office was planned to take place alongside the construction of Fallingwater, though work on the office quickly fell behind.

As Wilk notes, the office was the culmination of a "new geometric vocabulary" developed in Wright's ornamental designs in the 1920s

14 Secrest, *Frank Lloyd Wright*, 414.
15 Guerrero, *A Photographer's Journey*, 81.
16 Christopher Wilk, *Frank Lloyd Wright: The Kaufmann Office* (London: The Victoria & Albert Museum, 1993), 30.
17 For a thorough description of Kaufmann's activities in business and for the city of Pittsburgh, see Wilk, ibid., 27–30.

18 Ibid., 50.

19 Sandoval, letter to Wright, January 25, 1937. Wright Foundation Archives, Fiche ID: S050B10.

20 Sandoval, letter to Wright, April 21, 1936. Wright Foundation Archives, Fiche ID: S047A10.

21 Sandoval, letter to Wright, August 16, 1937. Wright Foundation Archives, Fiche ID: S053A01.

22 As Secrest notes: "Frank Loyd Wright was almost ludicrously inept when it came to handling money." Secrest, *Frank Lloyd Wright*, 35. Reflecting on Wright's work with Kaufmann, Wilk describes "a pattern repeated between Wright and many of his clients: an agreement by Wright to undertake the job; a long wait for designs; the client's urgent request for information and drawings; promises that the work is underway; delays; more urgent pleas; platitudes from Wright about the amount of energy he has put or will be putting into the project; requests for money from Wright; pleas from the client to start and finish the job within budget; etc." Wilk, *The Kaufmann Office*, 35.

and 30s.[18] His plan expanded Kaufmann's existing office and modeled its workings on a four-foot-square modular unit. The design's focal point was a plywood mural wall set above a large desk. The office included monumental, angled upholstered barrel chairs, low-slung stools, built-in storage units, integrated lighting, and louvered screens to diffuse the light from the room's exterior windows. The ceiling was composed of plywood panels that Sandoval "selected carefully, after a laborious manipulation so to produce a continuous efflorescence of cypress grain in the middle of the room running toward the desk below."[19]

Given the complexity of the office's carpentry, it is significant that Wright turned to Sandoval to realize his design. Accepting the offer to work on the project in April 1936, Sandoval sought to clearly establish the particulars of his employment and compensation—a reflection of his financial circumstances as he reestablished his shop in Chicago but also his past experience working with the notoriously tight-fisted architect.[20] Beginning in January 1937, Sandoval worked onsite in collaboration with two assistants, Ray Porras and another man by the last name of Barcenas, to realize every element of the office design. In mid-August, he informed Wright that work on the office was complete.[21]

Like many of Wright's projects, the Kaufmann office ended with cost overruns, disputes over finances, and recrimination.[22] In October, Wright wrote that Sandoval's handling of the project "looks crooked to me," criticizing him for hiring assistants, delays in minor adjustments to

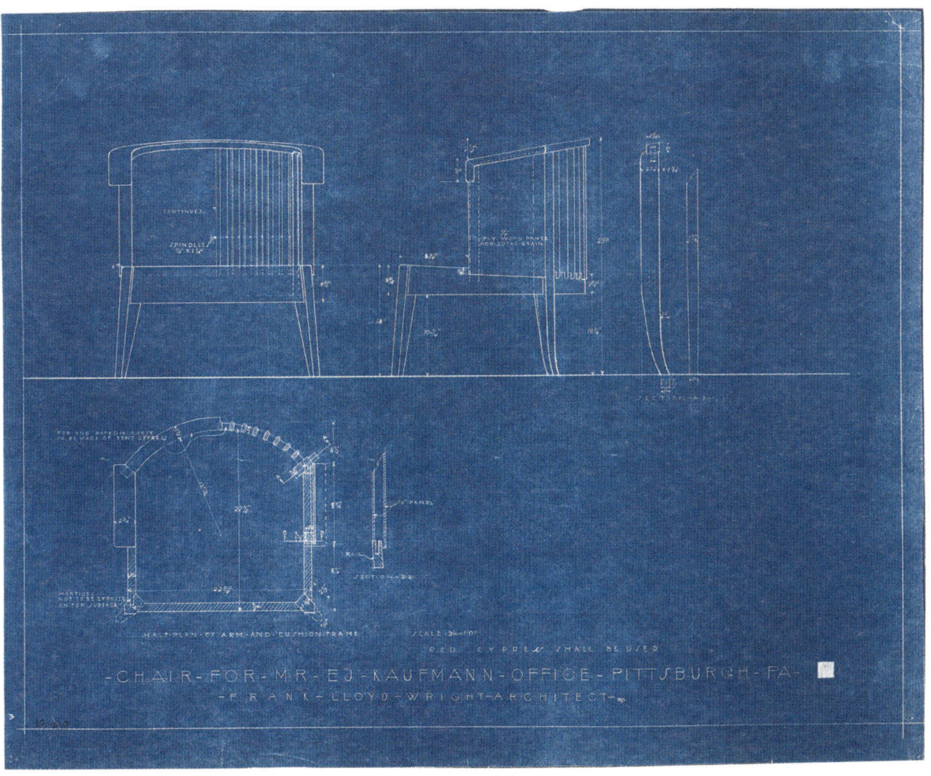

Frank Lloyd Wright, blueprint for Kaufmann office chair, 1937

the office's furniture, and bringing tools from the site home to Chicago instead of to Taliesin. "I say you owe us at least what you can do to get the work properly finished and some help up here [at Taliesin] to make what cash we have lost on you look like a good investment in a good friend. But maybe that isn't the way things work in Latin America."[23] Sandoval defended himself, replying that "so far as the Kaufmann job is concerned I feel that it was well done. I am a very particular person myself. I am proud of the work." He echoed the concerns he raised at the very beginning of the project: "About my going to Taliesen [*sic*]—I can return only if a salary commensurate with my ability can be agreed upon and definitely fixed . . . I have certain obligations (financial) which I cannot evade."[24] Wright replied bitterly: "What is offered to you now at Taliesin is much more than any salary would be and I see you don't understand what it is."[25] In addition to Wright's chronic refusal to acknowledge the financial and personal realities of his collaborators, the correspondence reflects how quickly race could be recruited to undermine Sandoval's place within the architect's circle.

Images of the Kaufmann office were first published in a special issue of *Architectural Forum* dedicated to Wright's work in January 1938. Conspicuously absent is any mention of Sandoval and his role in the creation of the office, something he protested to the architect and others.[26] Despite Wright's reticence to acknowledge his work, Sandoval had already left his own mark. On the underside of the office's massive desk, Sandoval and his collaborator Ray Porraz gave themselves credit for the labor that architectural history often denies. In pencil is a short note: "Manuel J. Sandoval & Ray Porraz. March 18/37, from Nicaragua and Guatemala C. America."

23 Wright, letter to Sandoval, October 14, 1937. Wright Foundation Archives, Fiche ID: S054A02.

24 Sandoval, letter to Wright, n.d. Wright Foundation Archives, Fiche ID: S054C01.

25 Wright, letter to Sandoval, October 20, 1937. Wright Foundation Archives, Fiche ID: S054A08.

26 Wilk, *The Kaufmann Office*, 71.

OFFICE FOR MR E J KAUFMANN PITTSBURGH PA
FRANK LLOYD WRIGHT ARCHITECT

Left:
Frank Lloyd Wright, blueprint for Kaufmann office relief mural, 1937

Right:
Kaufmann office interior, Pittsburgh, 1938

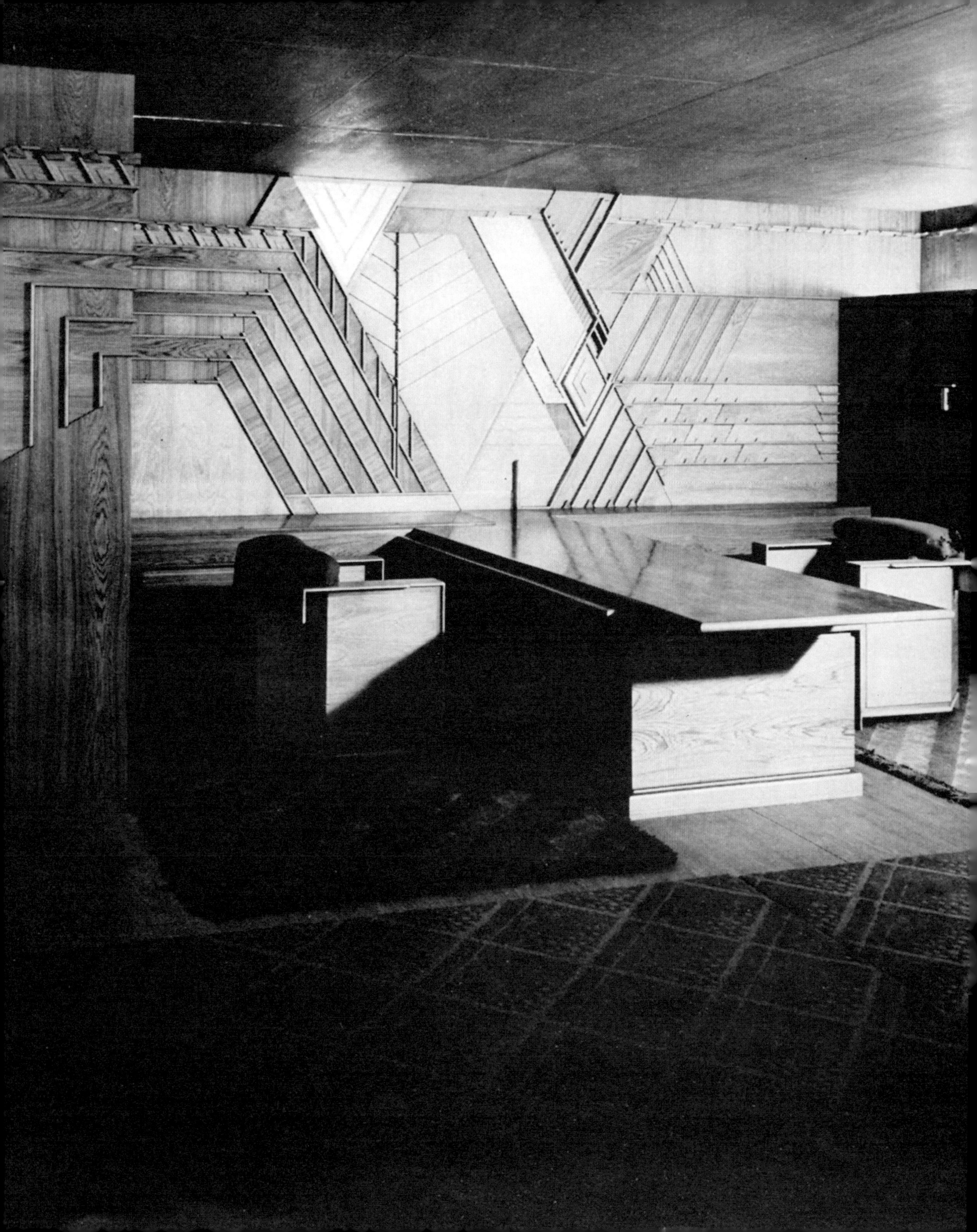

Later in his career, Sandoval would make relief murals much like the one in the Kaufmann office, filtering Wright's visual language through his own—in particular the geometries of ancient American art. Preciado does something similar in *So Near, So Far*, installing his own wall relief, desk, and pair of *Chumash chairs* (2019) together to evoke a corner of the Kaufmann office. Named for his own Chumash tribe and family, Preciado's chair creatively appropriates Børge Mogensen's Spanish chair—a Danish design inspired by Spanish colonial furniture—now viewed from an Indigenous perspective. Like Sandoval's murals or the pencil note hidden on the underside of Wright's desk, Preciado's office interior holds history open, inviting new layers of interpretation and use.

MODERNISM AND CRAFT
Los Angeles, California

Sometime in 1938, Sandoval relocated from Chicago to Los Angeles. In July, he wrote to Wright's assistant Eugene Masselink describing the challenges he faced establishing himself in a new city. "I have found out that in Los Angeles is [*sic*] very hard to find a job, either a good one or a bad one. I hardly have done anything since I came here, until last week I was fortunate enough to get one. Heavens knows how long it will last!"

Despite the disputes and allegations that emerged at the end of work on the Kaufmann office, Sandoval reflected on Wright and his work with nostalgia, noting that "by coincidence or love, the place where I'm working is located just about one half block from the Barnsdall place . . . I see from the street one of the buildings as I go to work everyday. It makes me feel that I'm always near our maestro."[27]

While the move represented a major change in Sandoval's life, Los Angeles was familiar ground for Wright and his circle of apprentices. Commissions in the city had helped launch a new stage of Wright's career in the 1920s, beginning with the Hollyhock House designed for Aline Barnsdall and continuing with projects like the Ennis and Storer houses. The West Coast also became a promising destination for Wright's apprentices, with the region's rapid growth providing opportunities to translate modern architectural vocabularies developed in Europe and the eastern United States to a new environment.[28] Wright's works in Southern California explored new possibilities—like the use of modular textile blocks and a visual language grounded in ancient Mesoamerican precedents, while California's climate offered greater opportunities to explore the integration of architecture with nature.

We know relatively little about Sandoval's life in Los Angeles. A series of addresses show him settling in the center of town, moving

27 Sandoval, letter to Eugene Masselink, July 11, 1938. Wright Foundation Archives, Fiche ID: S059D07.

28 As Elizabeth A. T. Smith describes, "Los Angeles during the early 1920s was on the cusp of a population explosion fueled by the advent of newcomers drawn by the promise of the oil and film industries, and was largely still unformed from a physical standpoint—a dispersed horizontal spread that offered great possibility in terms of the need for new construction and housing." See Smith, "R. M. Schindler: An Architecture of Invention and Intuition," in *The Architecture of R.M. Schindler* (Los Angeles: The Museum of Contemporary Art, Los Angeles, 2001), 25–28. Wright's apprentices who came to California to take advantage of these opportunities include Robert W. Beharka, Vincent Bonini, Loch Crane, Aaron Green, Frederick Liebhardt, Frederick Lothian Langhorst, Alvin Lustig, Sim Bruce Richards, R. M. Schindler, William E. Slatton, as well as Wright's own son, Lloyd Wright.

29 Jay Oles notes that most of the Mayan
Revival architecture in late-nineteenth
and early-twentieth century Los Angeles
was done by white architects and designers who "elevated distant (and lost)
indigenous cultures while ignoring the
political rights of more local (and living)
indigenous peoples." In this respect,
Sandoval was unique in being a Latin
American designer who contributed
to California's fascination with the
ancient Americas. See Oles, "Reviving
the Pre-Hispanic Past: From Mexico to
California," in *Design in California and
Mexico: 1915–1985*, Wendy Kaplan,
ed. (Los Angeles: Los Angeles County
Museum of Art, 2017), 127.

30 Vance Bourjaily, "Cabinet-Maker Works
Wonders in Wood," *San Francisco
Chronicle*, May 28, 1950, 3L. Bourjaily's
invocation of "primitive" Latin American
art speaks to the art history of his time
and its reflection of racist logics, further
reflected in the depth of the perceived sep-
aration between works of modern design
and those that drew on other traditions.

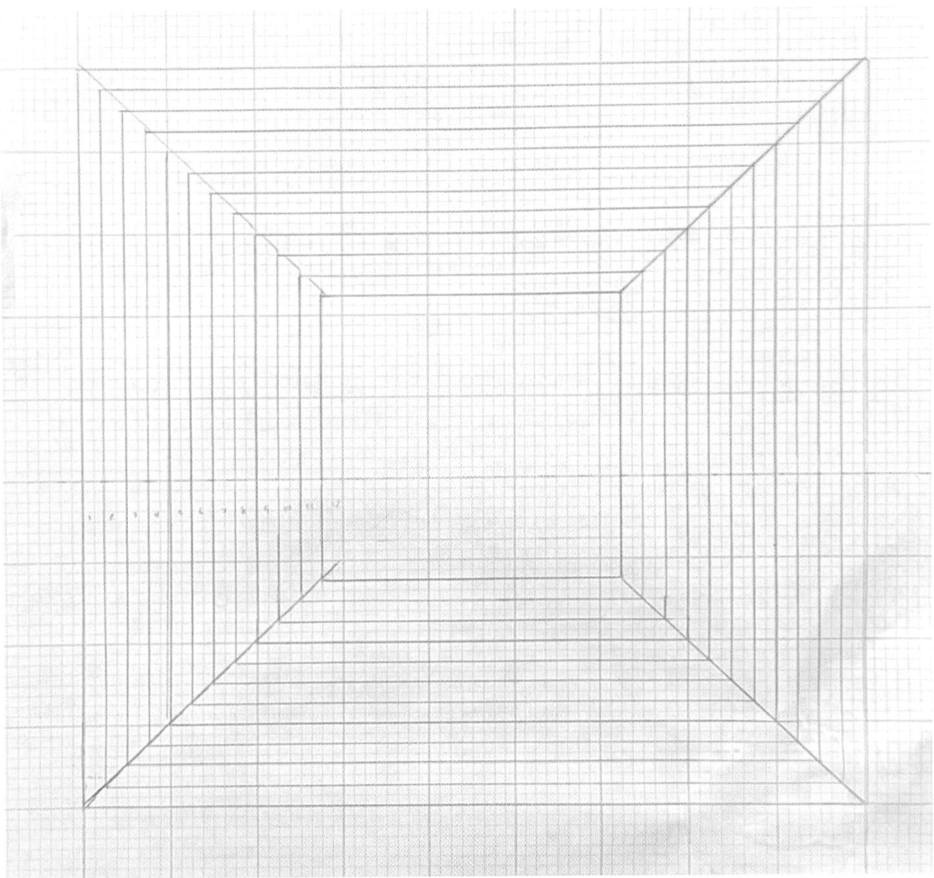

Ryan Preciado, study for *Second
Nature*, 2024

occasionally within the same Pico-Union neighborhood. It seems that
during this period, he returned to his own furniture practice, working in
a Mayan Revival style especially popular in Los Angeles at the time.[29]
Sandoval's interest in exploring ancient American precedents through
his furniture was longstanding. He recalled "doing intricate wood carvings in the manner of the Mayans" by the age of seventeen. Some of his
mature works resonated with Wright's own Mayan Revival architecture
in Los Angeles, but others speak more closely to a Latin American folk
art tradition, reflecting a lived connection to an ancient heritage different from the appropriations and pastiches more common in work by
white American designers at the time. As one commentator described,
in Sandoval's furniture, "the rich decorative feeling of primitive Latin-
American art and the structural simplicity of modern design are both
present—sometimes reconciled and sometimes not."[30]

Sandoval reappears in the architectural archive only through his
work with other Wright apprentices in the city. In the mid-1940s, he
renewed contact with architect and graphic designer Alvin Lustig—
another former Taliesin fellow whose short time there overlapped
with Sandoval's—building cabinetry, furniture, and room screens for
Lustig's Beverly Hills office (1944–46). As Lustig's assistant at the

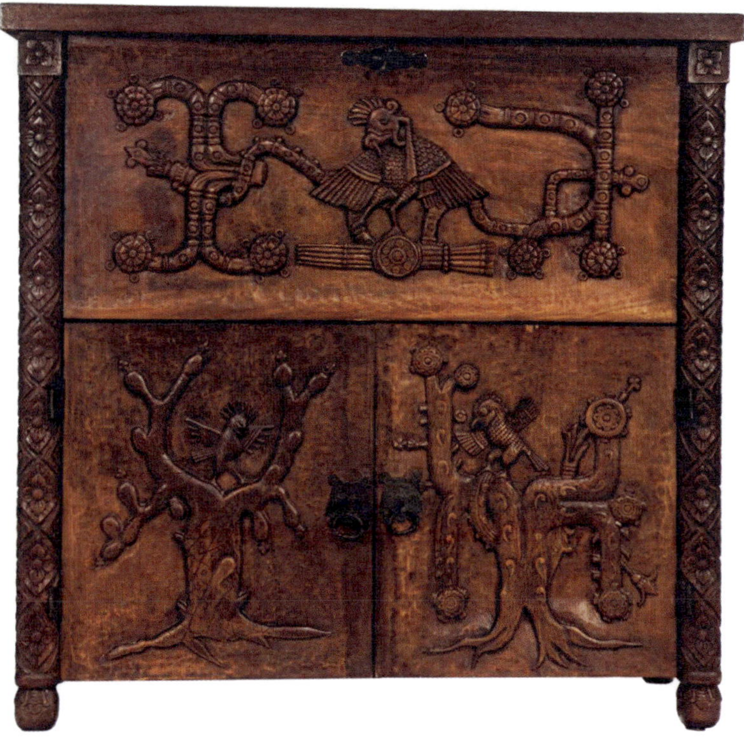

31 Interview with Ken Parkhurst, quoted in Andrew Romano, "Meet Manuel Sandoval," *The Lustig House*, February 26, 2014. While difficult to attribute with certainty, Romano notes that it is possible that Sandoval did other work for Lustig during this period.

32 At this time, Wright himself was largely in Japan overseeing work on the Imperial Hotel in Tokyo. Schindler would himself design key elements of the Barnsdall Complex (now the Barnsdall Art Park), including the Director's House (Residence A) for an envisioned artist retreat there.

33 Schindler, quoted in Esther McCoy, *Five California Architects* (New York: Reinhold, 1960; repr. Los Angeles: Hennessy + Ingalls, 1985), 151. Citation refers to the Hennessy + Ingalls edition.

34 R. M. Schindler, "Furniture and the Modern House: A Theory of Interior Design (Part 1)," *Architect and Engineer*, vol. 123 (December 1935): 22–25; repr. in Marla C. Berns, ed., *The Furniture of R. M. Schindler* (Santa Barbara, CA: University Art Museum, University of California, Santa Barbara, 1997), 43. Citation refers to the University Art Museum edition.

35 David Gebhard, *Schindler* (New York: Thames & Hudson, 1971; repr. San Francisco: William Stout, 1997), 145. Citation refers to the William Stout edition.

time described, "It was done in genuine mahogany. It was breathtakingly beautifully done. The guy was a master."[31]

Around the same time, he was hired by Schindler, another former Wright collaborator in Los Angeles. After joining Wright's office in 1918, the Austrian emigré had moved to California in 1920 to oversee construction of the Barnsdall House, a relocation that would prove permanent.[32] Schindler's work with Wright had brought the same frustrations Sandoval and others would later experience in the fellowship. His pay was low and inconsistent, and he experienced the same outbursts that Sandoval encountered in his work on the Kaufmann office. Perhaps most importantly, Schindler found that Wright's domineering character stifled the design voices of his apprentices. Writing to a friend, Schindler once complained that "Not one of Wright's men has yet found a word to say for himself."[33]

Despite this, Schindler articulated a vision of architecture that echoed Wright's commitment to the *Gesamtkunstwerk*—what Schindler called "space architecture." He argued that "the space architect, sees the house as an organism in which every detail, including the furniture, is related to the whole and to the idea which is its source."[34] As David Gerhard notes, Schindler "had to be intimately involved in every aspect of design and construction," often making purposefully loose architectural drawings that "left him free to improvise and design, not in the drawing office but on the site."[35]

Manuel Sandoval, desk, 1938

36 David Gebhard and Patricia Gebhard, "The Furniture of R.M. Schindler," in *The Furniture of R. M. Schindler*, 25. See also Gebhard, *Schindler*, 129. As Gebhard describes, Schindler "designed more and more of his furniture in plywood in such a way that it could easily be built by the carpenter on the job, rather than by a cabinetmaker."

37 See Gebhard and Gebhard, "Furniture of Schindler," 33.

38 Schindler, letter to Sandoval, April 4, 1946. R. M. Schindler Papers, Architecture and Design Collection, Art, Design & Architecture Museum, University of California, Santa Barbara, Project Files: Bigelman House, 22/19 IV.B.

This embrace of an improvisatory approach to design is reflected in Schindler's furniture. His expressive-but-spare modernism embraced materials like plywood and corrugated plastic as well as the efficiencies of modern construction. Much of his early furniture catered to the skills of the American contractor and the scraps left over from construction, comprising works in plywood that sometimes showed a "lack of concern for the rudiments of construction."[36]

Schindler had turned to Sandoval to recreate furniture first developed in the 1930s for the Van Patten (1934–35) and Walker (1935–36) houses as part of his renovation of the home of Dr. Leo and Zara Bigelman (1944–47). The dining set reflects Schindler's commitment to furnishings that were low and light. Both the table and chairs float on their I-beam supports.[37] However, unlike much of his other furniture, these designs required the skill of a carpenter like Sandoval. They were structurally complex and used Russian ash much finer than his usual plywood.

It was Preciado's own effort to produce this complicated furniture that began his dialogue with Sandoval and his story in 2020. While the work of reproduction is rare for Preciado, the task of faithfully recreating Sandoval's work prompted interest not just in his tools and techniques but also the knowledge, skill, and life that lay behind them. From this experience, Preciado took new technical and formal interests (the skeletal structure of his *Toro table* echoes Schindler's design as much as the work of Carlo Mollino) but also a desire to reconstruct Sandoval's story, to bring it into his making as much as the designs of his architect collaborators.

Unfortunately, Sandoval's experience with Schindler ended much like his work on the Kaufmann office. Surviving correspondence between Schindler and Sandoval shows similar disputes over the timing and cost of the project. In early 1936, Schindler excoriated Sandoval over delays in making the furniture, threatening legal action to enforce their initial agreement. Sandoval noted that the price Schindler and Bigleman were willing to pay for his labor ($200) represented less than a third of his usual rate. Schindler dismissively replied, "Your present rates are of no interest," eventually agreeing to pay half of Sandoval's standard fee.[38]

Schindler's undervaluing of Sandoval's labor and expertise may be explained by the former's own understanding of furniture as the product not of expert hands but of the architect's vision working through accessible and inexpensive means. This attitude was hardly unique in the context of California modernism, where an exploration of mass production, modularity, and efficiencies of construction helped inaugurate a new kind of American architecture more distant from the world of craft. Unlike Wright's architecture—influenced by the Arts and Crafts movement and still dedicated to work by hand

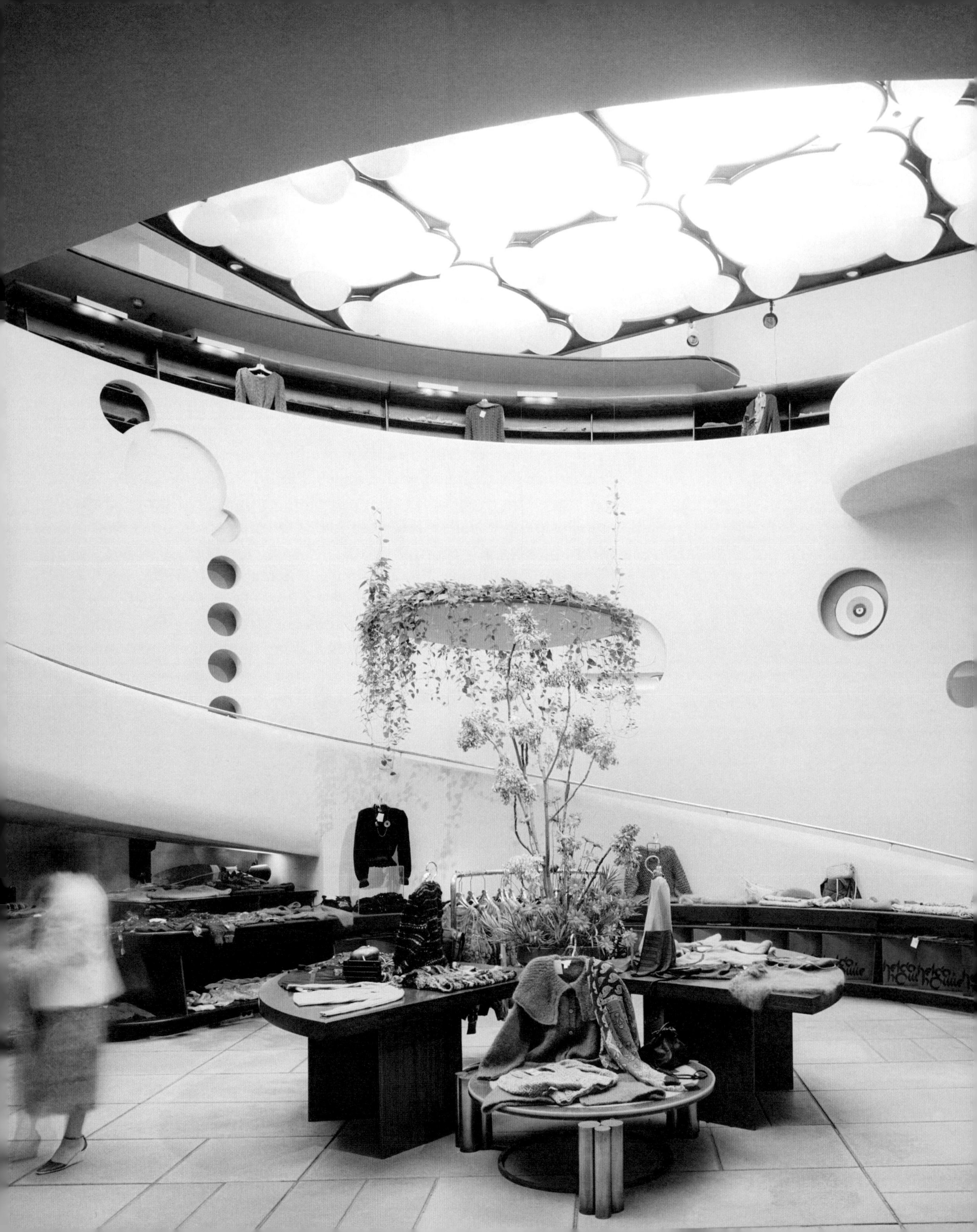

39 Esther McCoy, "Ticul Pottery," *Los Angeles Times Home Magazine* (April 29, 1956): 32. See Robert J. Kett, "Where Is Yucatan? Julius Shulman at Chichen Itza," *Getty Iris*, January 12, 2015: https://blogs.getty.edu/iris/where-is-yucatan-julius-shulman-at-chichen-itza/.

40 Curtis Besinger, *Working with Mr. Wright: What it Was Like* (Cambridge, EN: Cambridge University Press, 1997), 190.

41 Elizabeth B. Mock, quoted in "China and Gift Shop by Frank Lloyd Wright for V.C. Morris," *Architectural Forum* (February 1950): 80.

42 Wilk, *The Kaufmann Office*, 21.

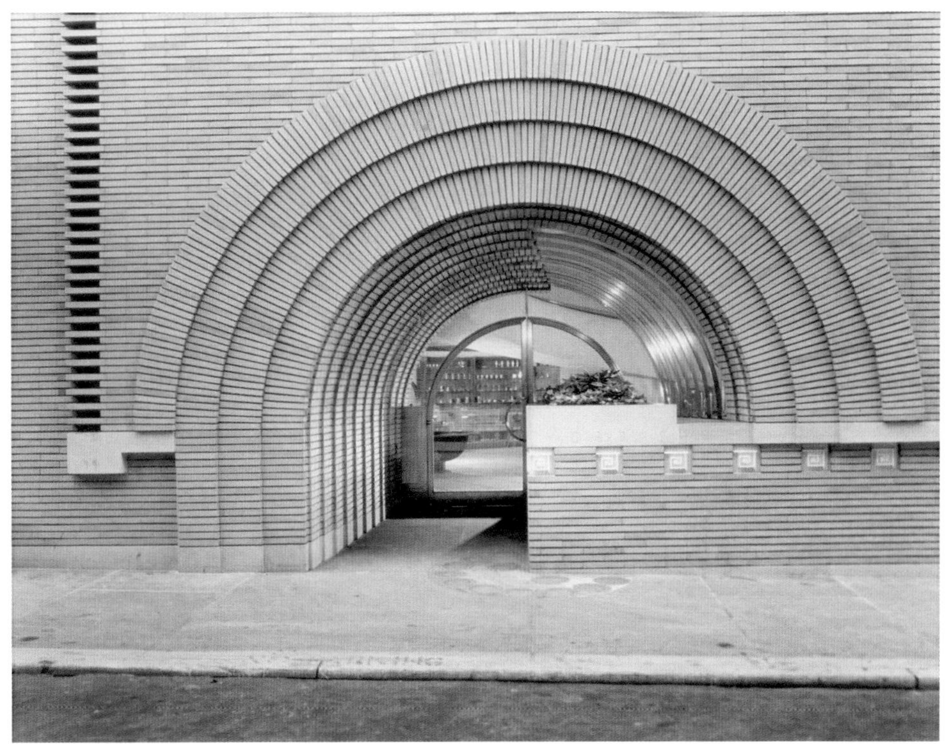

Left:
V. C. Morris Gift Shop interior, San Francisco, 1933

Right:
Frank Lloyd Wright, V.C. Morris Gift Shop exterior, 1951

in the age of the machine—in California modernism craft became an accessory that offered "an individual note" increasingly seen as the work of Others.[39]

LEGACIES
San Francisco, California

In 1948, after years of being out of contact, Wright "began a search for Manuel Sandoval."[40] The carpenter's work on the Kaufmann office and relocation to California made him an ideal collaborator for a new project—the reinvention of an existing structure on San Francisco's Maiden Lane as a shop for V. C. Morris, an art and design gallery.

Wright's design rehearsed an enduring fascination with architectural compression and release. Fronted by a blank brick rectangular facade with an arched doorway, the visitor was denied the usual translucency of retail exteriors, eventually entering an interior that offered a dynamic experience of curvilinear space built off of a central ramp. As Elizabeth Bauer Mock noted when the project was first published in *Architectural Forum*, "The circular spiral of the ramp is the pervading theme, developed in endless variation: reduced to disk or hole, elongated as cylinder or tube, blown into domes and spheres."[41] Wright had long been interested in the ramp as a design conceit and alternative to traditional forms of circulation.[42] It would reappear in his last major building for the Solomon R. Guggenheim Museum in New York. However, the V. C. Morris Gift Shop was the first opportunity he had to realize this vision.

These variations on the ramp's curves were realized through elements like the building's ceiling, which filtered natural light through a field of inverted plastic domes, but also through circular and crescent-shaped furniture and cabinetry. Sandoval was instrumental in translating the architectural cues of Wright's organic architecture into a layered and functional interior. Wright apprentice John deKoven Hill recalled that "everything was all designed, beautifully executed by Manuel Sandoval . . . it was more like seeing jewelry sort of assemble itself."[43]

43 John deKoven Hill, interview, Frank Lloyd Wright Oral History Program, n.d., UCLA Library, Center for Oral History Research.

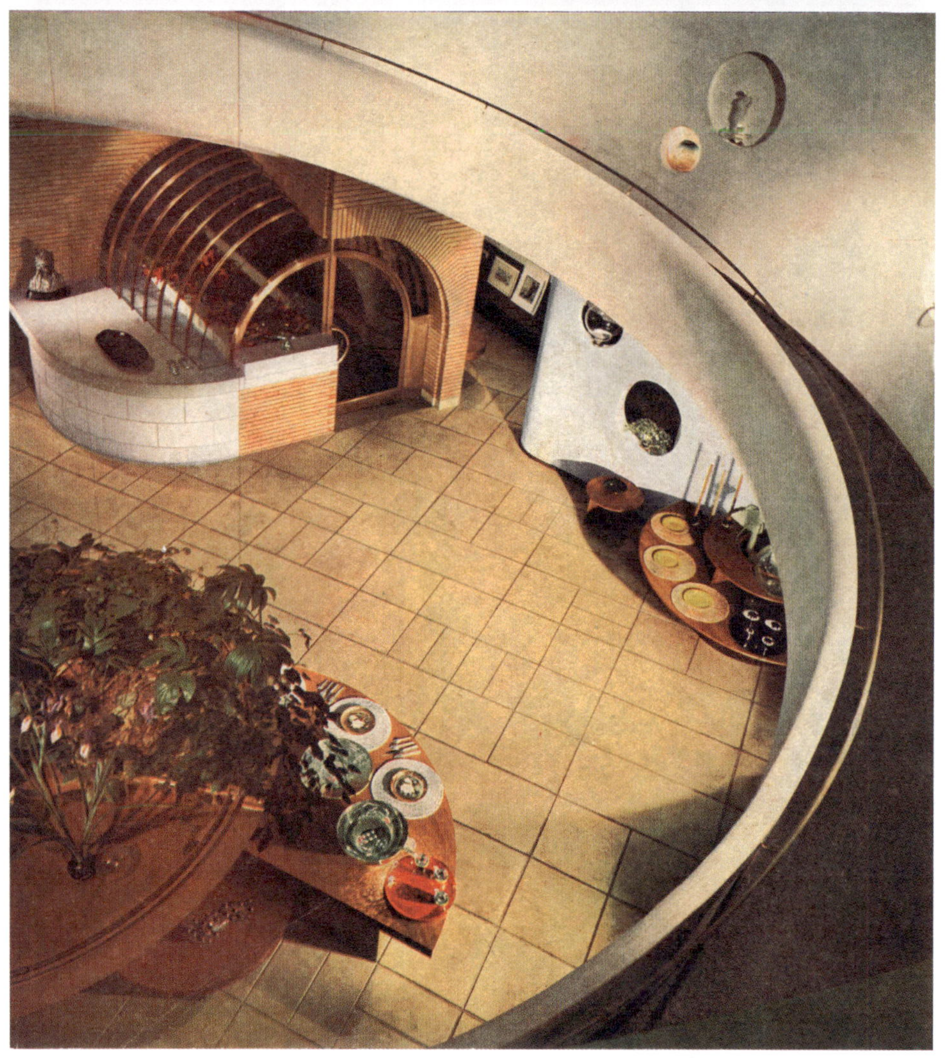

Cover, *Architectural Forum*, February 1950

44 Reese Palley, "Wright as an educator," *Pacifica Radio*, June 8, 1969.

45 Sandoval, letter to Wright, September 1, 1948. Wright Foundation Archives, Fiche ID: S159D09.

46 Bourjaily, "Cabinet-Maker Works Wonders in Wood," 3L.

Reflecting on a later restoration of the space in the 1960s, the gallerist Reese Palley described uncovering Sandoval's "acres of beautifully, meticulously finished walnut" that "glowed like a violin case."[44]

Melding the materiality and dynamic forms of Sandoval's furniture with Wright's orthogonal frame for the V. C. Morris shop building, Preciado's *Sandoval Stool* (2024) is a rectangular volume perforated by crescent openings and containing curved arms that suggest the pent-up motion of an armillary sphere. A building in miniature, the stool reverses Wright's reduction of furniture to a simple reflection of architecture, speaking instead to how Sandoval's work allowed Wright's design language to function at the scale of interiors and bodies.

For Sandoval, the return to collaborating with his mentor on the V. C. Morris shop was invigorating. In a letter to Wright, he wrote: "Once again I find myself in the road to freedom away from routinary work so common in cities like Los Angeles. This particular work I'm now doing has elevated me once again to the days when I was with you." Sandoval closed his last surviving letter to Wright by affirming, "I remain your faithful disciple."[45]

Like all of his experiences working with Wright, Sandoval's involvement in this project proved transformational. He closed his shop in Los Angeles and relocated to San Francisco, opening a studio on Dolores Street. In 1949, he created cabinetry for Wright's Maynard Buehler House (1948–49) in Orinda, California, his last-known collaboration with his complicated mentor.

While records of Sandoval's time in Los Angeles document frustration, it seems that the Bay Area was professionally and personally stimulating. He had steady work making furniture and cabinetry for local architects like Fred Langhorst, another fellow during Sandoval's time at Taliesin. In 1950, he was profiled in the *San Francisco Chronicle* in an article celebrating the relocation of "one of the best cabinet-makers in North America" to the city. The author notes that in addition to furniture, Sandoval "likes to paint, draw, design interiors and houses." His furniture continued to meld ancient American forms with modernist design, while at the heart of his studio was a large-scale "cabinet-maker's mural" of angled geometries whose patterns could be rearranged by moving its pieces. Beside a photograph of Sandoval's mural in the article is an image of his realization of Wright's design for the Kaufmann office. The juxtaposition is a visual testament to Sandoval's labors for Wright but also his own reinvention of the architect's design language.[46] Sandoval continued to work in his own unique idiom for the rest of his life, later reestablishing his studio in Los Angeles and eventually retiring in Escondido.

It is hard to reconcile Sandoval's devotion to Wright with the self-importance and cruelty the architect often shows in their correspondence. But the former's commitment seems real. Edgar Tafel remembers a velvet-lined box Sandoval once created to store a pencil the architect had given him, a reflection of his "reverence for Mr. Wright."[47] Reverence was a common enough sentiment among fellows as they navigated the strange mix of mentorship and power in Wright's studio. However, Sandoval's marginality within the fellowship itself speaks to what was different about his experience, how race and the racialization of craft have left him outside the usual accounts of Wright's architectural lineage. But it is also what is unique about Sandoval and his work. Instead of remaining at Taliesin and seeking to echo the voice of his "maestro" in architecture, and despite limitations imposed by the racism of his time, he persevered in navigating professional opportunity and his own craft.

The silences that persist in Sandoval's story point to a larger, unwritten chapter in the history of the built environment, detailing the lives and labor of those architectural workers forced—whether by racism, sexism, classism, or other structural inequities—to the margins of the field. Preciado's work in *So Near, So Far* marks these absences but also fills them with his own inferences and interventions. Moving beyond the task of recreation that first introduced him to Sandoval's story, Preciado's new works undermine a commitment to individual architectural authorship, contributing instead to a more expansive, ongoing design dialogue that includes Wright, Sandoval, himself, and others. These objects include a design for an imagined velvet-lined pencil box (*Atentamente*, 2024) and the *Sandoval Stool*. Like Sandoval, Preciado offers his own response to Wright's mural in the Kaufmann office—the young artist's iteration grounded in a new sense of identity, time, and place. These works are tributes to Sandoval, creative offerings that stand in for absences in history's more formal archive. They also demonstrate that what history has neglected need not be a dead end—rather, it can become an opening for a new kind of making that embraces the collective nature of the creative process.

47 Tafel, *Apprentice to Genius*, 85.

The caption on the left margin:

Vance Bourjaily, profile of Manuel Sandoval, "Cabinet-Maker Works Wonders in Wood," *San Francisco Chronicle*, May 28, 1950

Cabinet-Maker Works Wonders in Wood

Frank Lloyd Wright Is Among Fans

ONE OF THE BEST cabinet-makers in North America has set up shop in San Francisco.

He is Manuel J. Sandoval, and the recommendation comes — by inference at least—from no less a source than Frank Lloyd Wright.

Twice Wright has called Sandoval in to execute the woodwork plans for important commercial jobs: first for the Kaufman department store in Pittsburgh, and more recently for the V. C. Morris store in San Francisco's Maiden lane.

Another distinguished architect, somewhat more available to off-hand telephone inquiries than Wright, is Fred Langhorst, who is currently making use of Sandoval for a home in Hillsborough. Langhorst calls the cabinet-maker: "One of the most talented men in his field that I know."

Those who have visited the Morris store and have seen the beautifully fashioned, dark wood shelves which curve about its circular showroom will probably agree.

A Nicaraguan

Sandoval was born in Nicaragua, the son of a carpenter, and learned his father's trade. By the time he was 17, he remembers, he was doing intricate wood carvings in the manner of the Mayans. In furniture which Sandoval designs himself, the rich decorative feeling of primitive Latin-American art and the structural simplicity of modern design are both present—sometimes reconciled and sometimes not.

In the early 1930's, Sandoval was in Chicago, working in the construction trade and studying architecture at night. He went one day to see an exhibit of Wright's work, and was very much impressed. A short time later he learned of Wright's colony of students and architects in Wisconsin and wired, offering his services as a carpenter and his enthusiasm for learning architecture.

Wright, whom Sandoval says has great respect for people who can work with their hands, wired back and told him to come ahead.

The association lasted several years, with Sandoval doing much of the Wisconsin carpentry and carrying out assignments for various of Wright's clients. When the Kaufman job was done, Sandoval says: "Mr. Wright told me, 'As a businessman, Sandy, you're not much, but as an artist I take off my hat to you.' It is wonderful when a great master like that says such a thing."

Painting, Designing

Sandoval opened a cabinet shop in Los Angeles and stayed ten years, interrupting his business for a few months to join Wright's group at Taliesin West in Arizona. He closed the Los Angeles shop finally to come here and do the Morris work, liked San Francisco and stayed on.

In his shop on Dolores street Sandoval is working at the furnishings Langhorst has designed for the Hillsborough home, and designing furniture on his own. Besides cabinet-making he likes to paint, draw, design interiors and houses. Mostly, though, he is occupied with his trade.

Into the small rooms of his apartment, a few blocks from the shop, Sandoval has wedged much of the furniture he once made for larger quarters in the South. There are tables and chairs, a sleek radio-phonograph cabinet, lamps, shelves, benches and panes of glass with varnish over odd designs in watercolor—suggesting illuminated finger paintings.

Of all the work in the room, Sandoval is proudest of a panel of wood which occupies the center of one wall. It is a cabinet-maker's mural, executed on a flat board with a mechanical saw. Most of the pattern is executed in series of parallel grooves, set at angles to one another. Smaller pieces of wood are arranged in patterns across the surface, fitted into the grooves in such a way that the pattern can be changed by changing their positions.
            —*Vance Bourjaily*

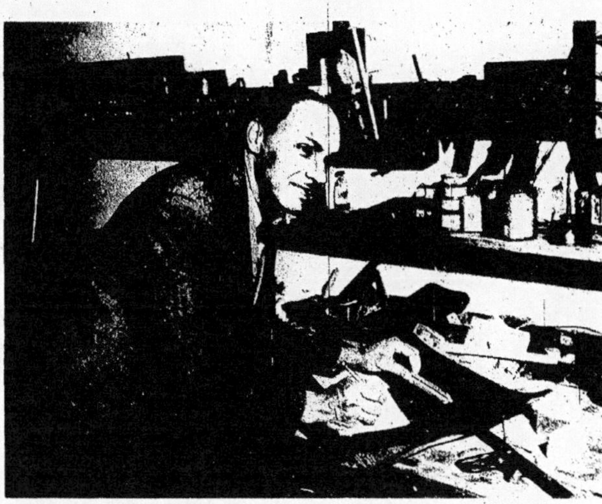

MANUEL J. SANDOVAL, native of Nicaragua and one of the most noted U. S. cabinet-makers, works on furniture in his San Francisco shop. Besides working wonders in wood, he paints, draws, designs interiors and houses.

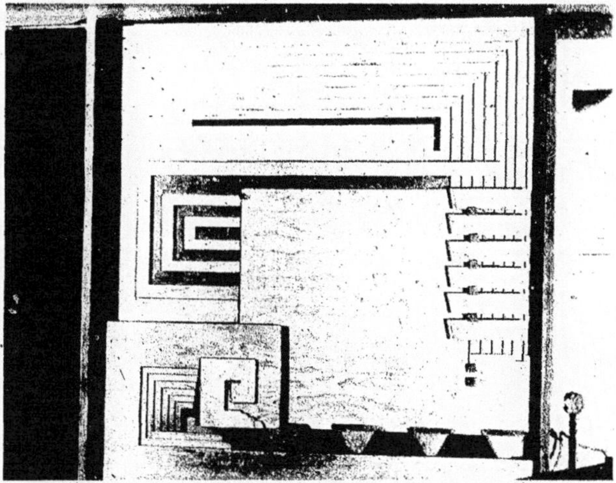

SANDOVAL IS PROUD of a panel on a wall in his own apartment. It's a cabinet-maker's mural executed on a flat board with a mechanical saw. Most of it is executed in a series of parallel grooves.

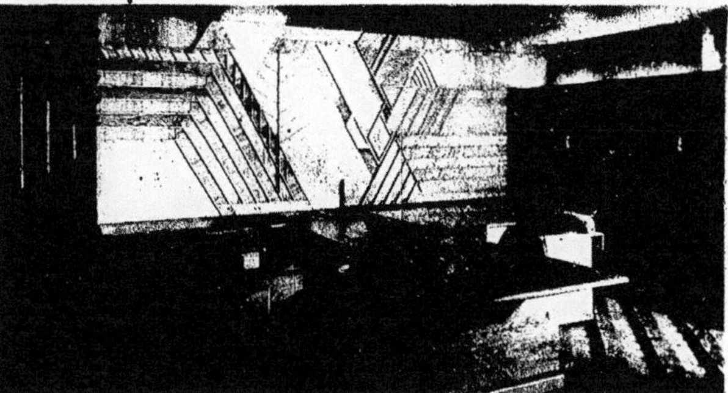

EXECUTIVE OFFICES of Philadelphia's Kaufman Department Store (shown here) contain examples of Sandoval's work. More recently he has done interior jobs for Frank Lloyd Wright's V. C. Morris store in Maiden Lane.

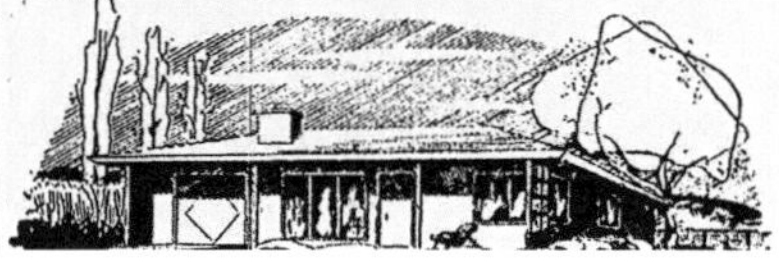

So Near, So Far

Sandoval Stool, 2024
Lacquer on red oak and wool
19 × 16 × 16 in. (48.3 × 40.6 × 40.6 cm)

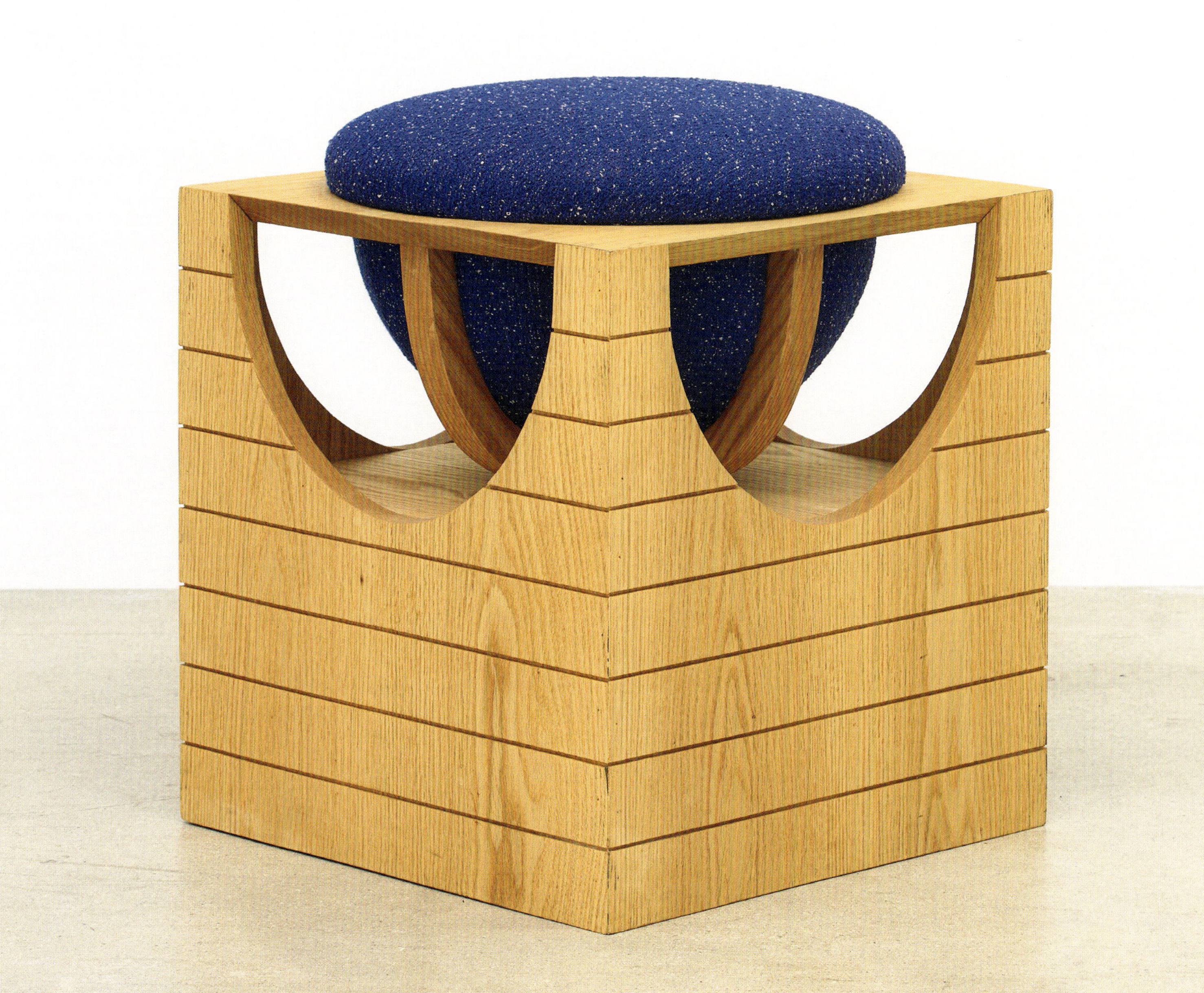

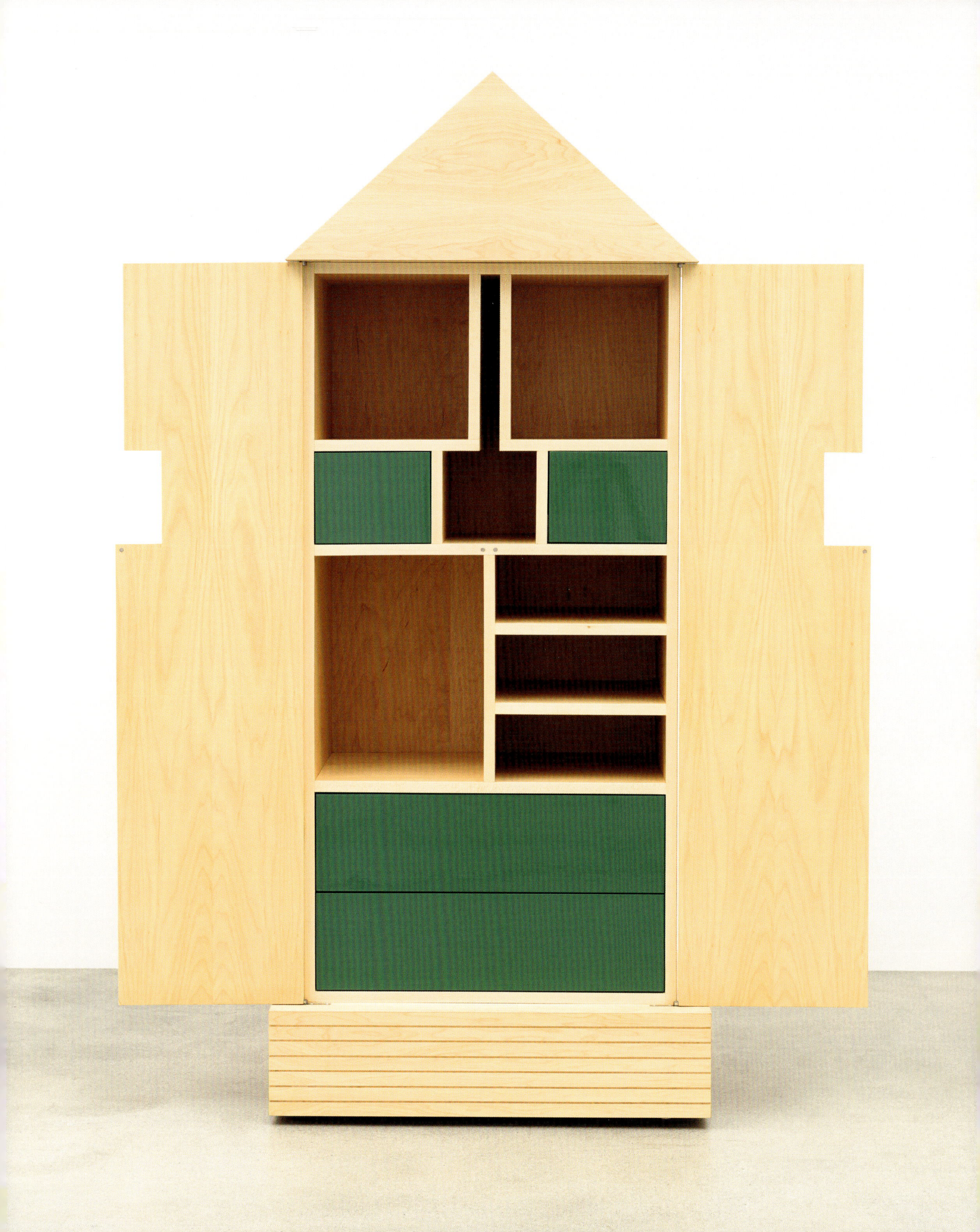

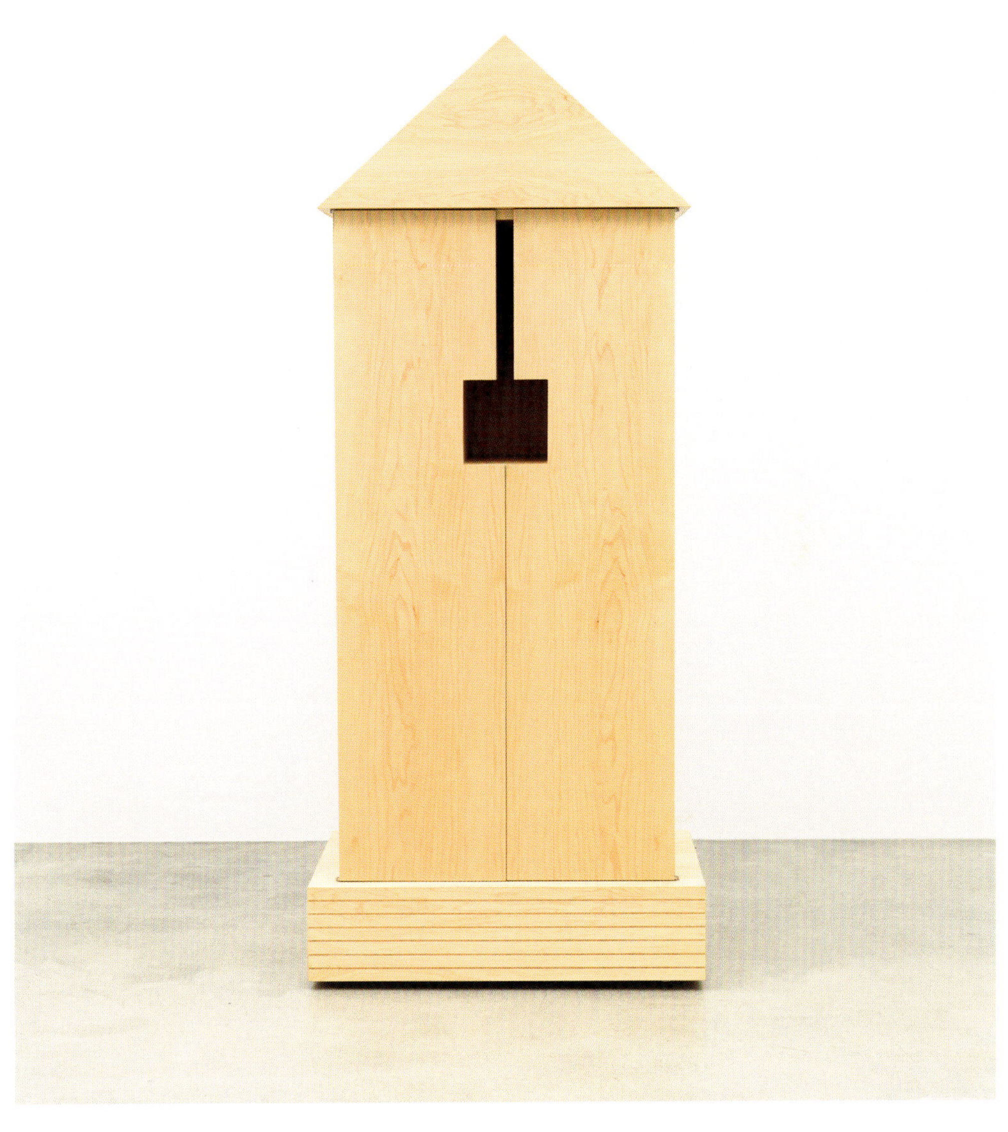

Oceano Cabinet, 2023
Automotive paint on maple, maple veneer, and plywood
66¾ × 28⅛ × 21¼ in. (169.5 × 71.4 × 54 cm)

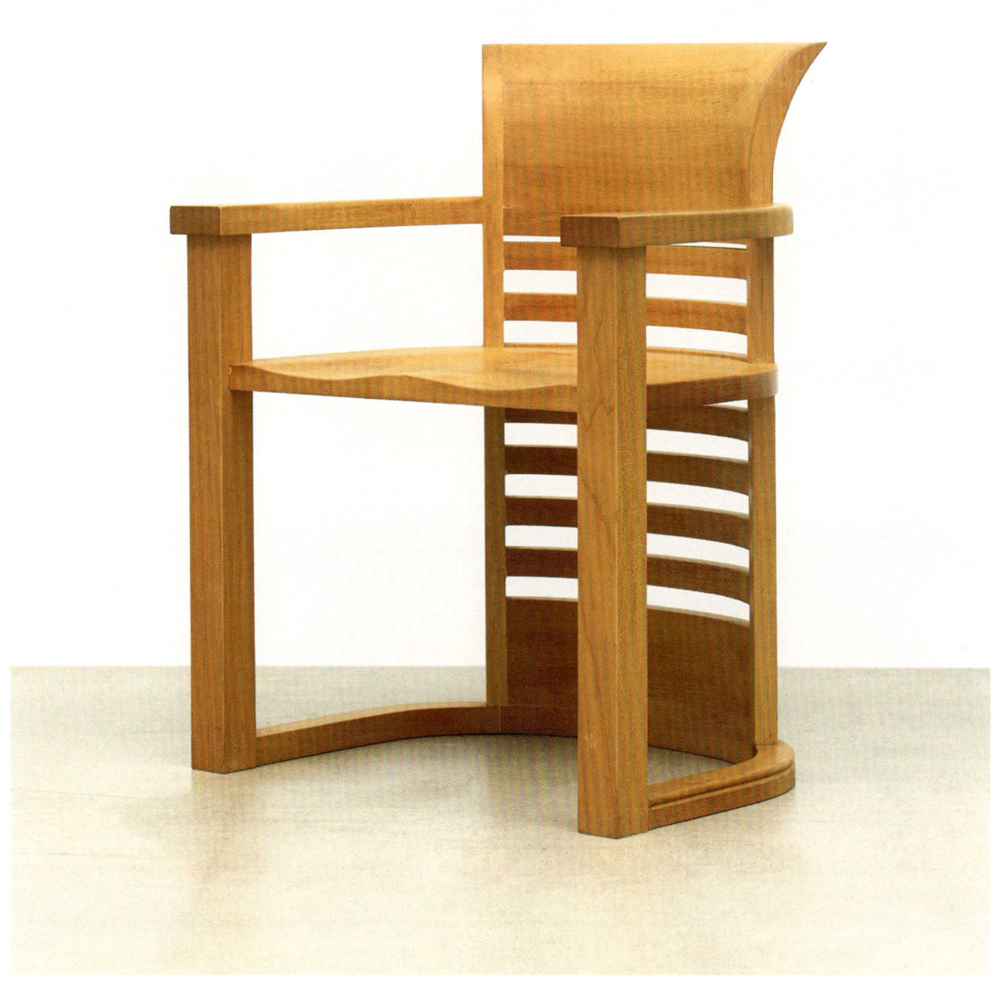

138 Chair, 2022
Maple
31⅜ × 24⅝ × 21⅛ in. (79.7 × 62.6 × 53.7 cm)

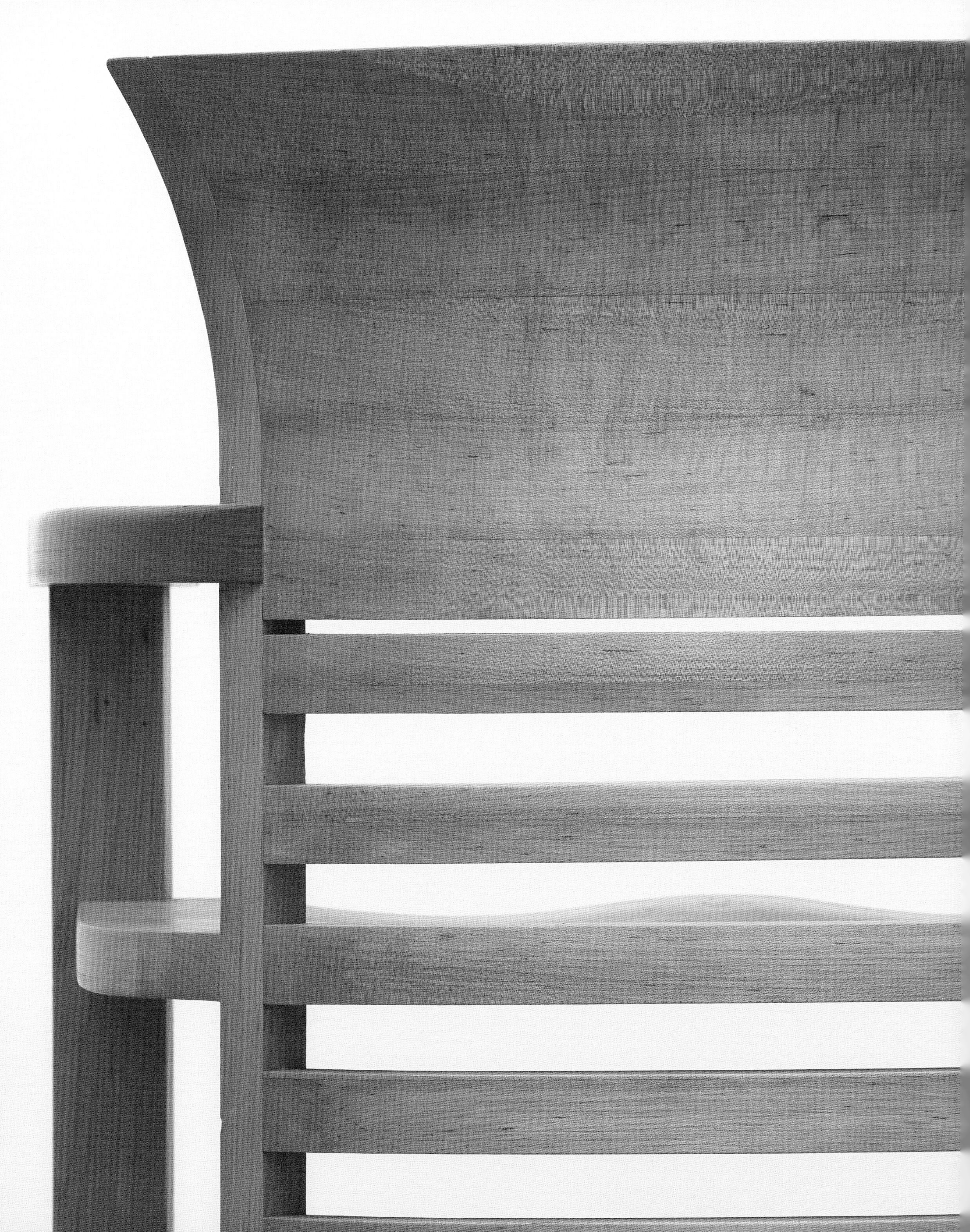

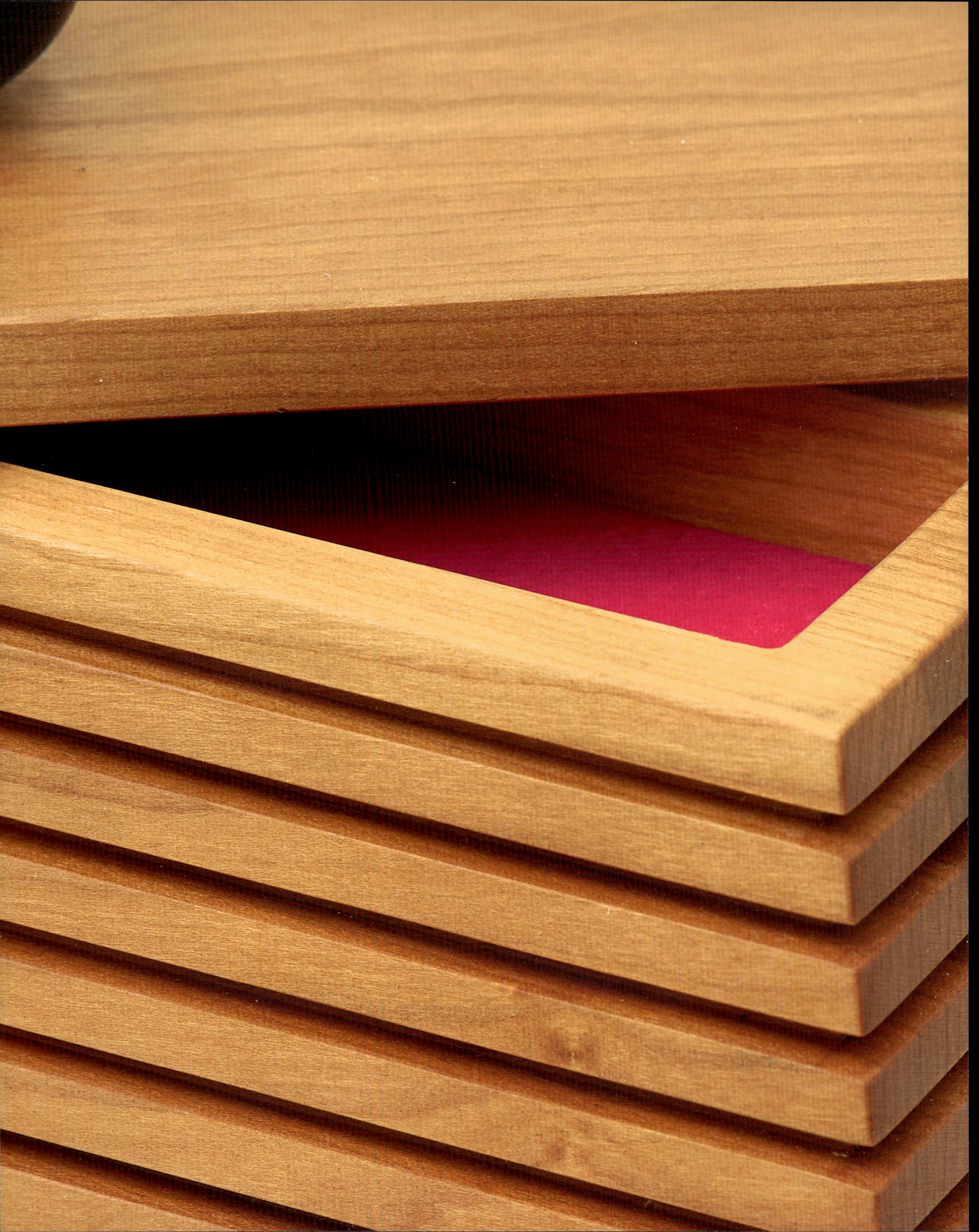

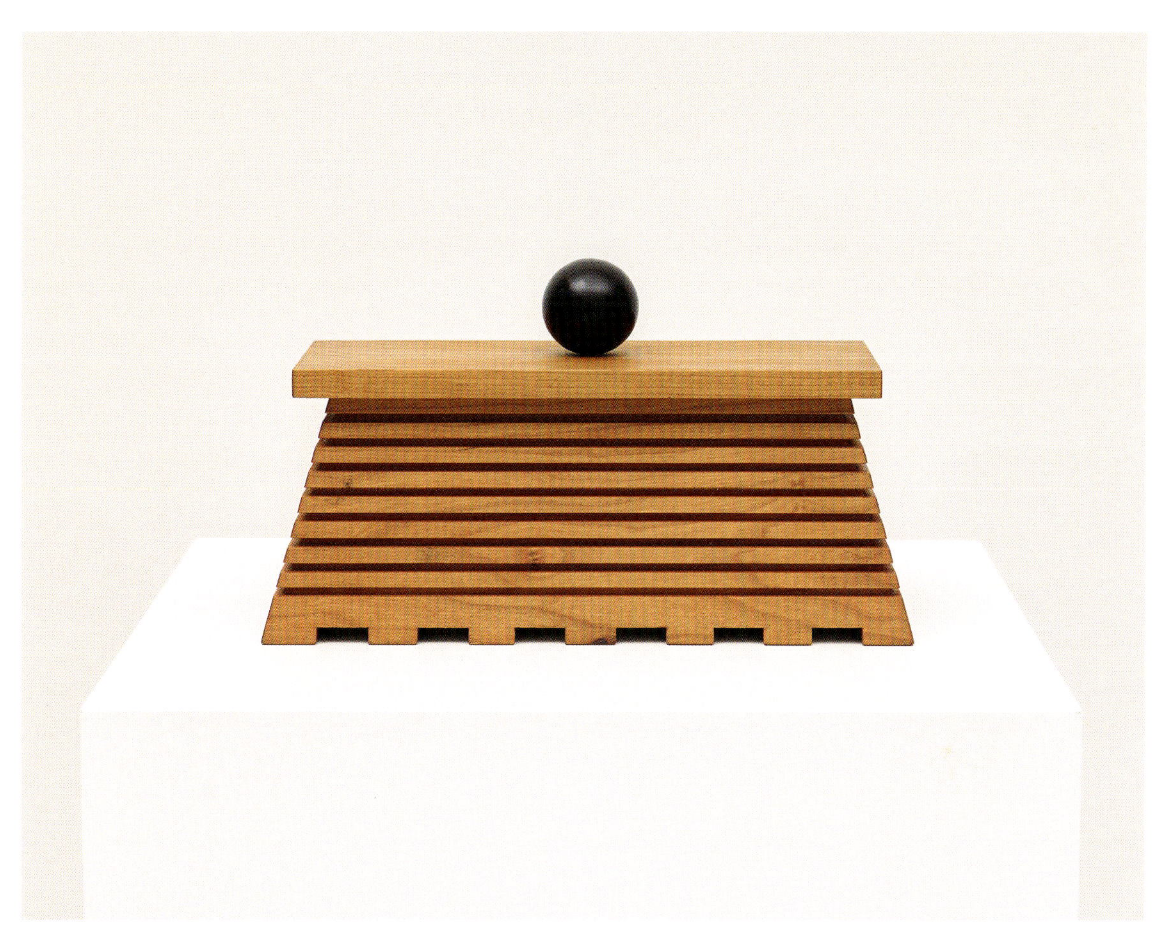

Atentamente, 2024
Felt and lacquer on cherry and alder
5¾ × 9⅞ × 5 in. (14.6 × 25.1 × 12.7 cm)

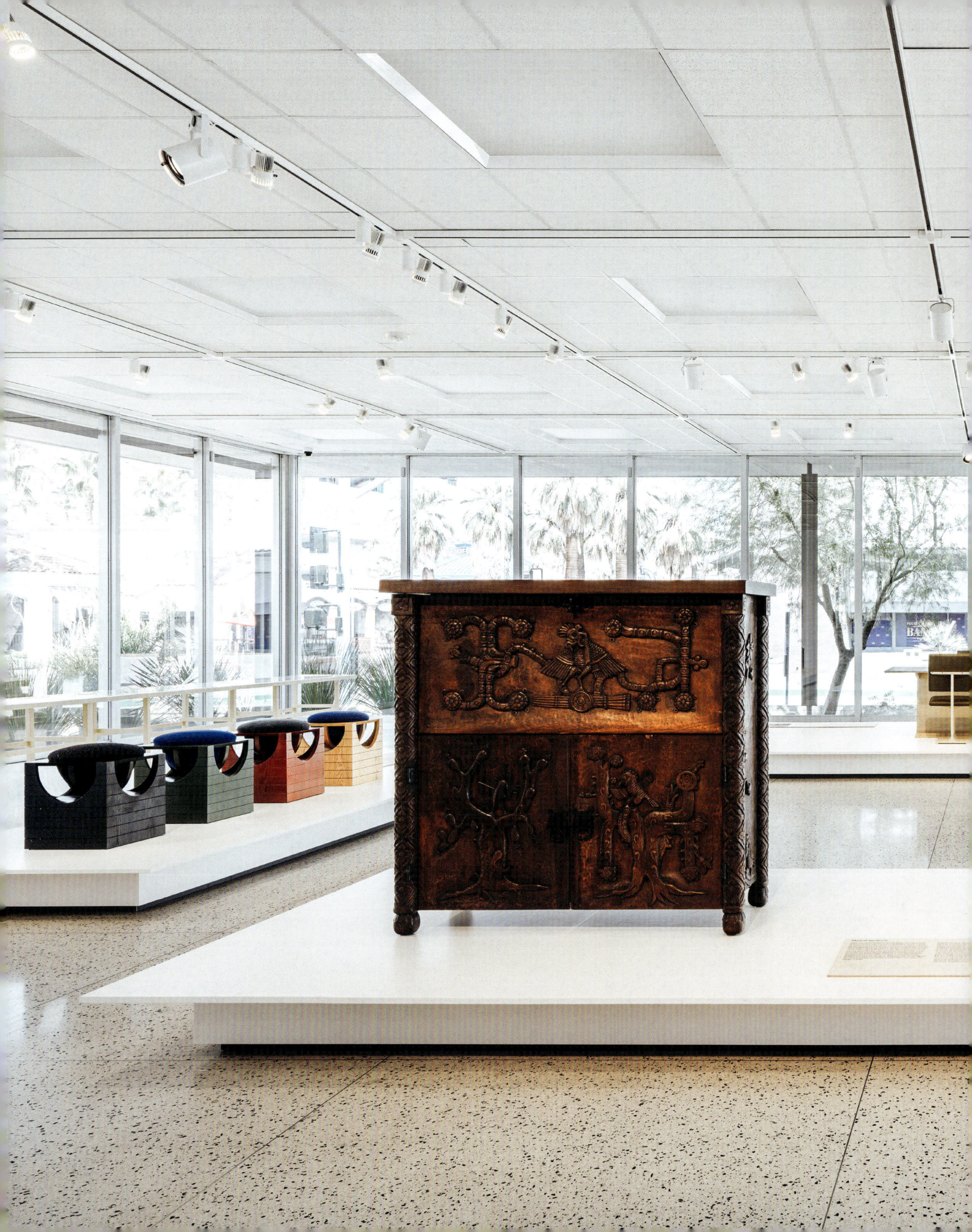

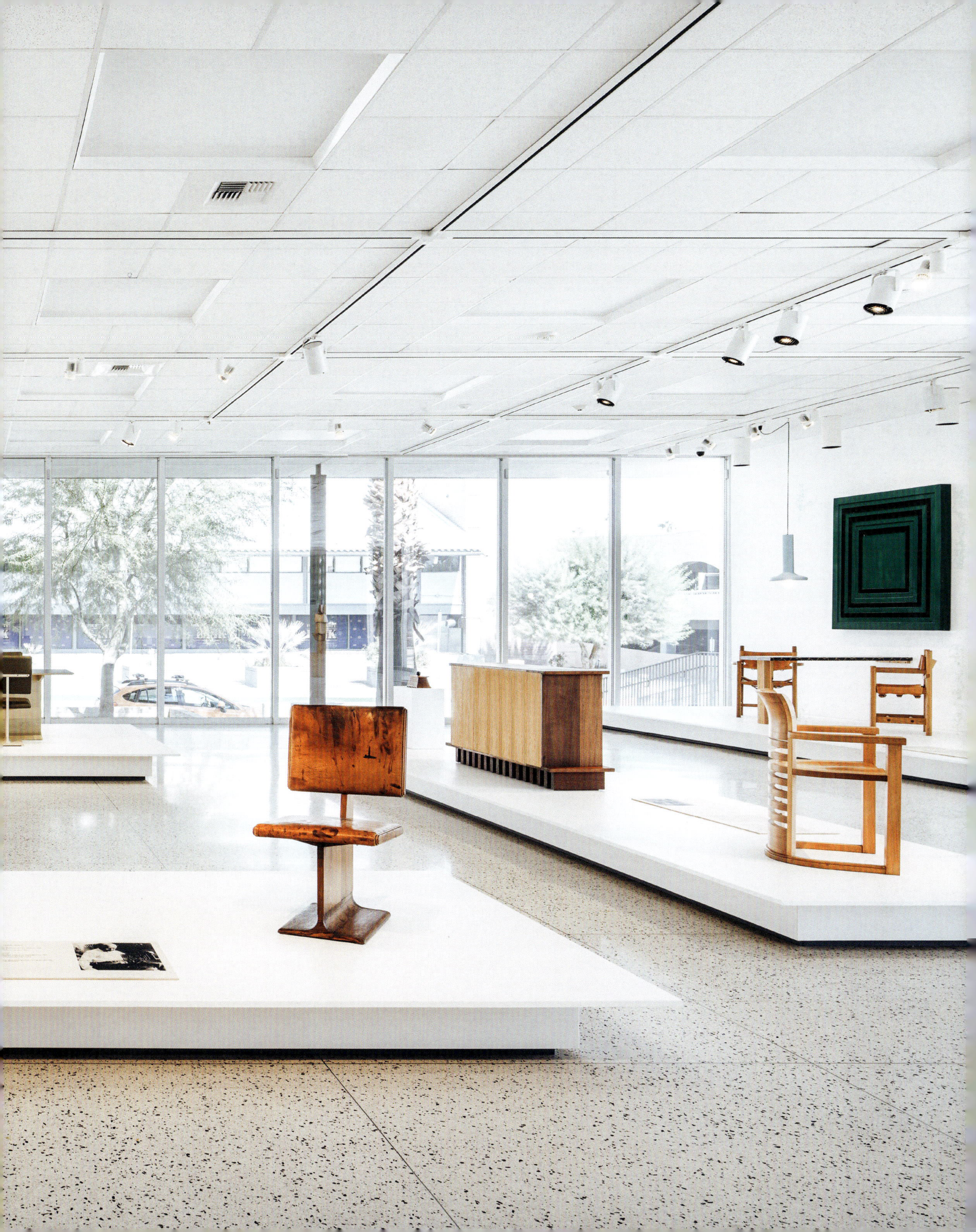

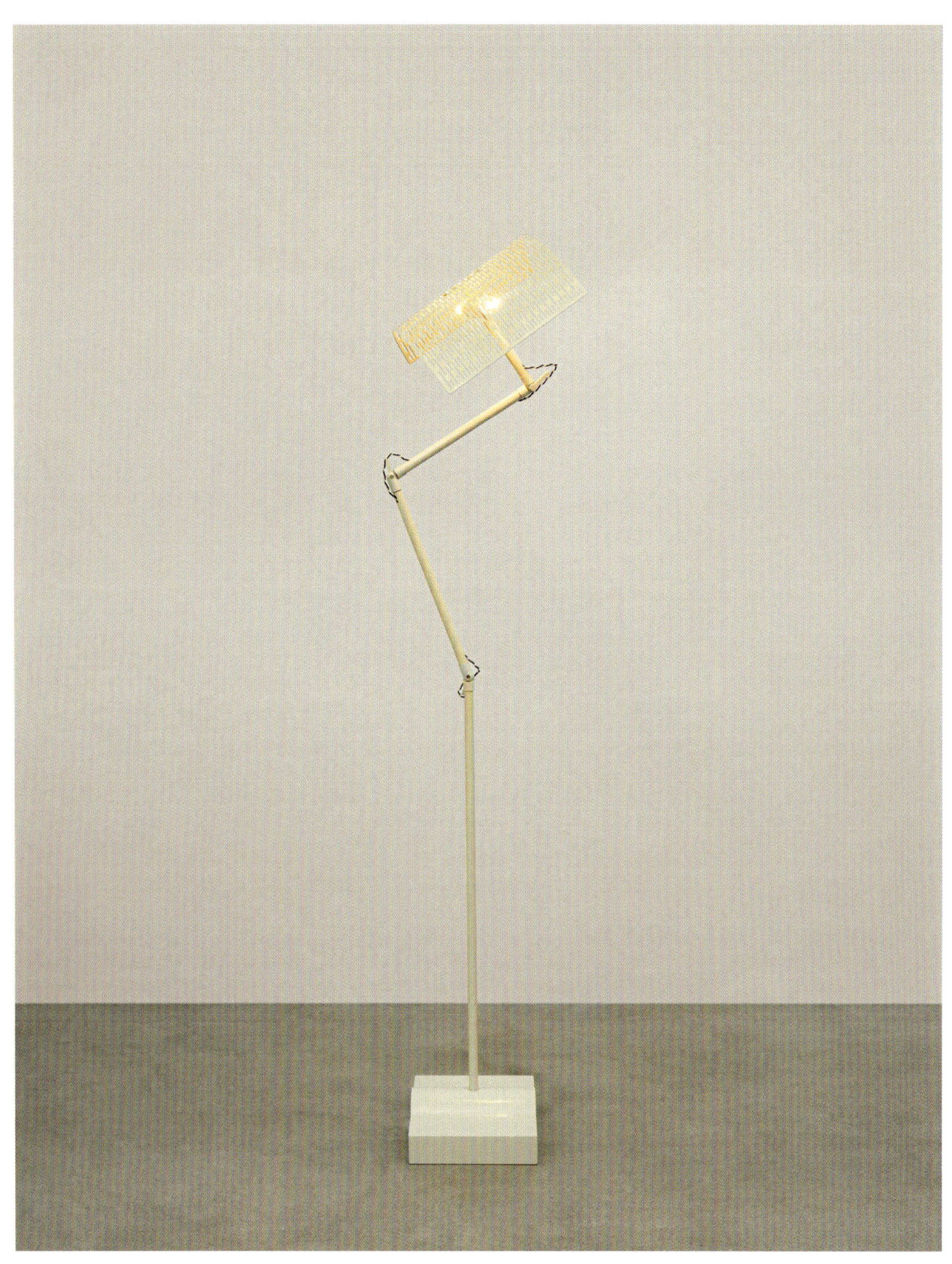

Duke of Earl (Floor Lamp), 2023
Powder-coated aluminum and steel
63 × 15 × 15 in. (160 × 38.1 x 38.1 cm)

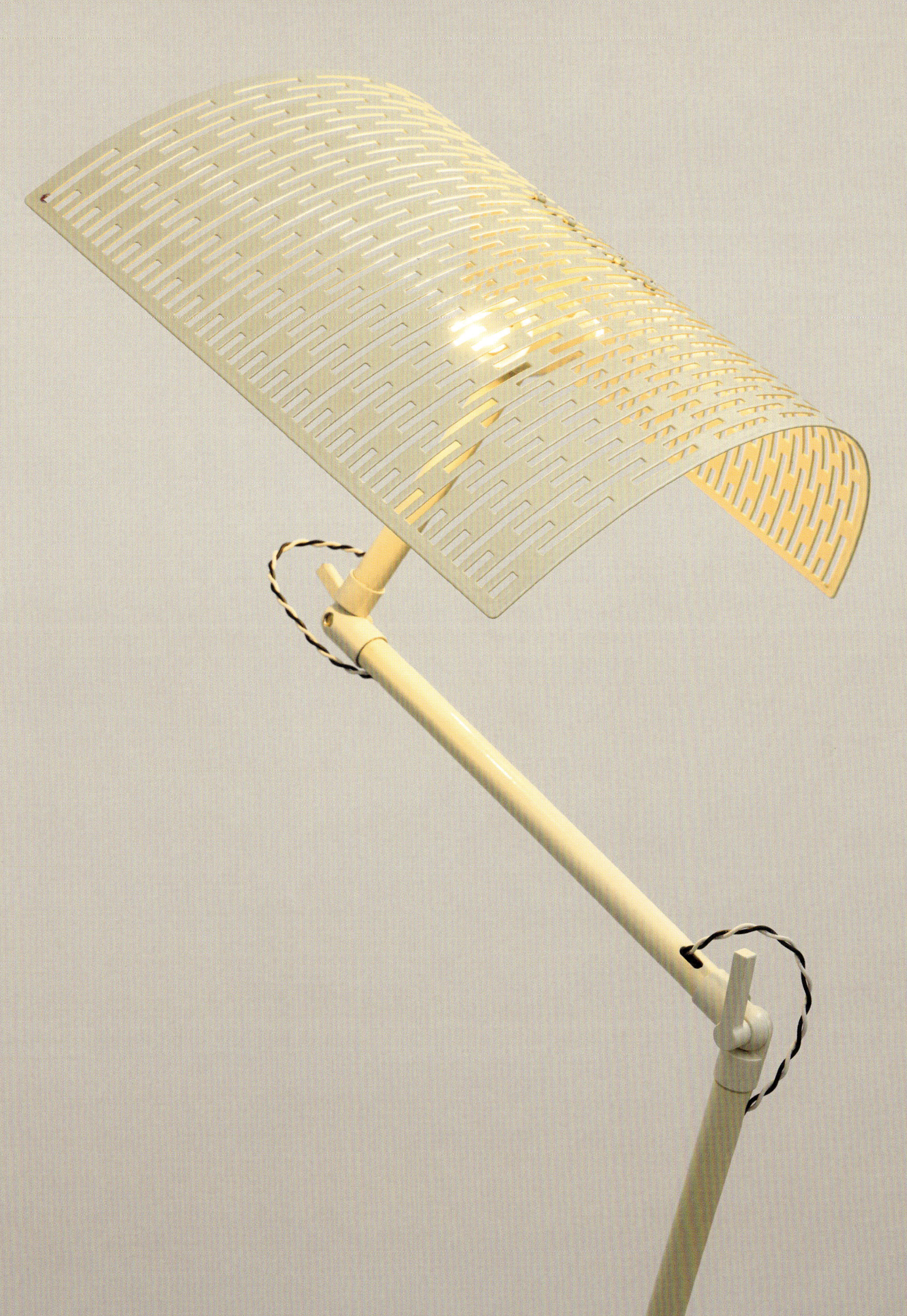

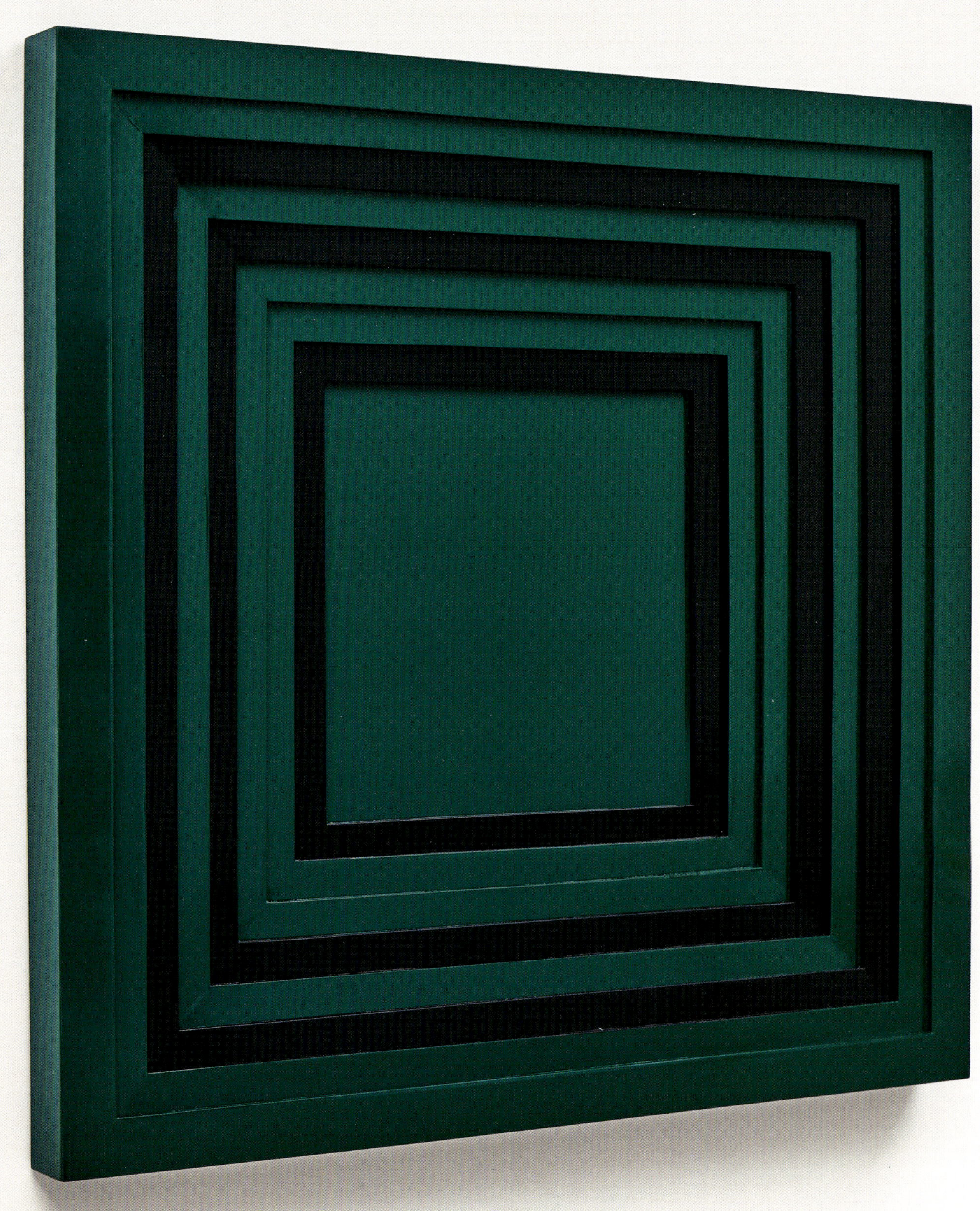

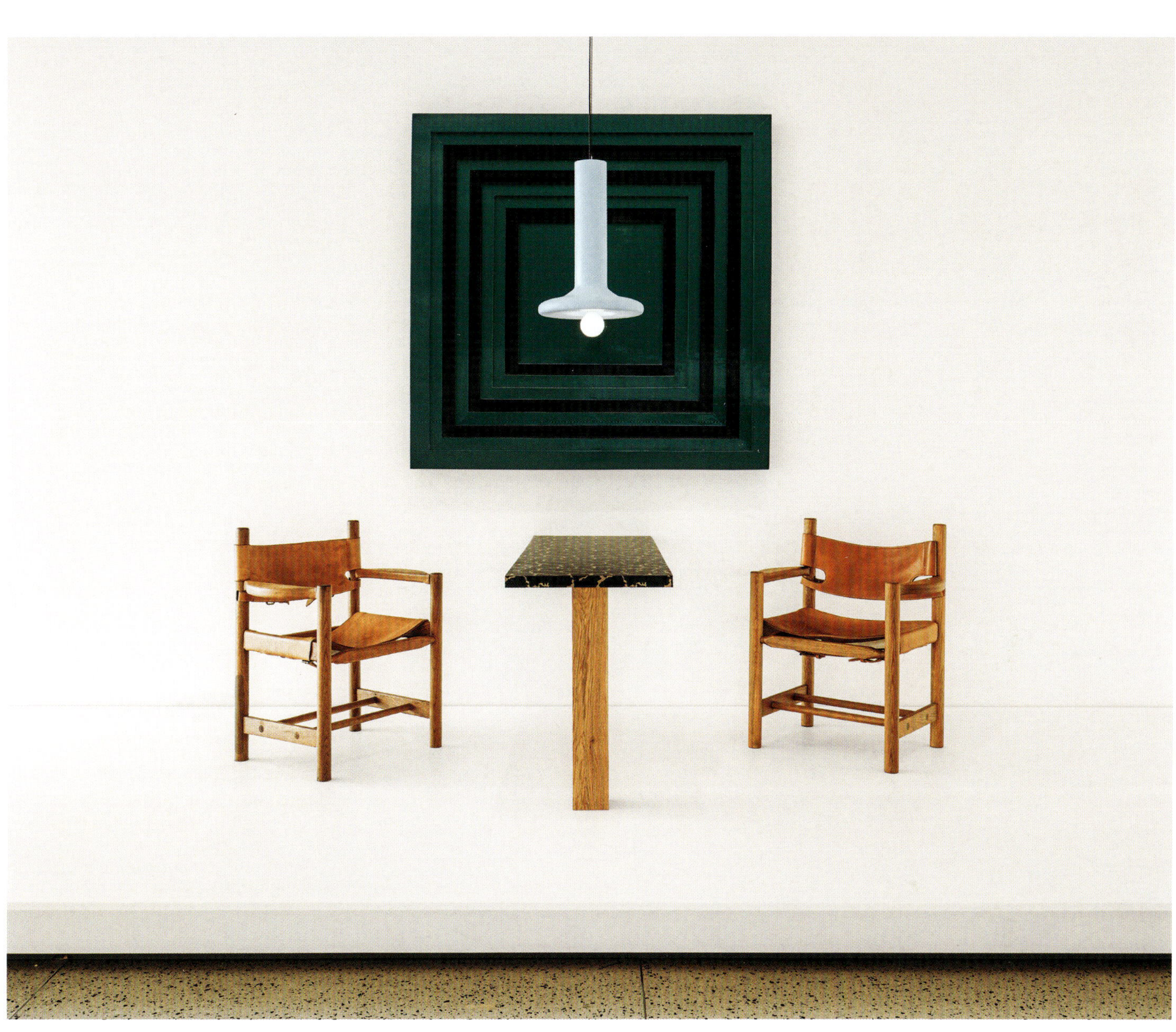

Second Nature, 2024
Automotive paint on plywood
60 × 60 × 4 in. (152.4 × 152.4 × 10.2 cm)

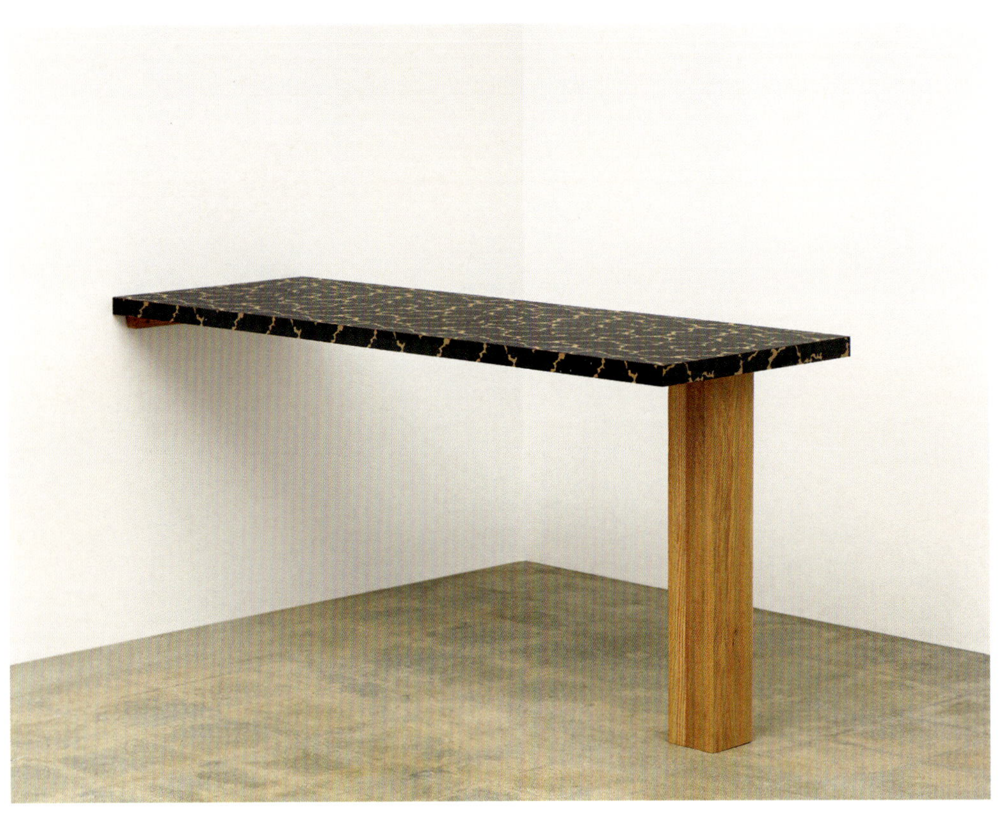

Plank Table, 2024
Laminate on plywood and white oak
29½ × 60 × 20 in. (74.9 × 152.4 × 50.8 cm)

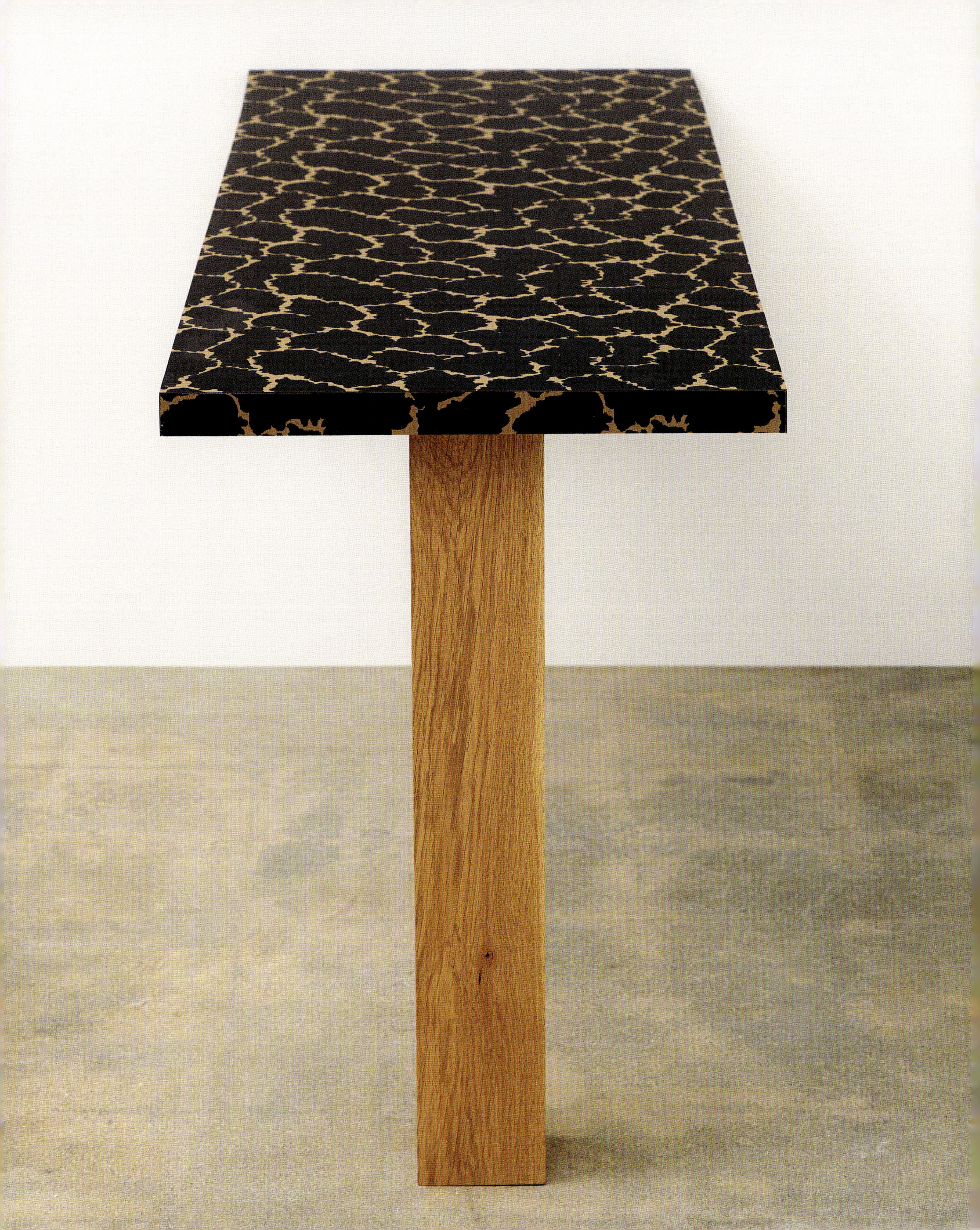

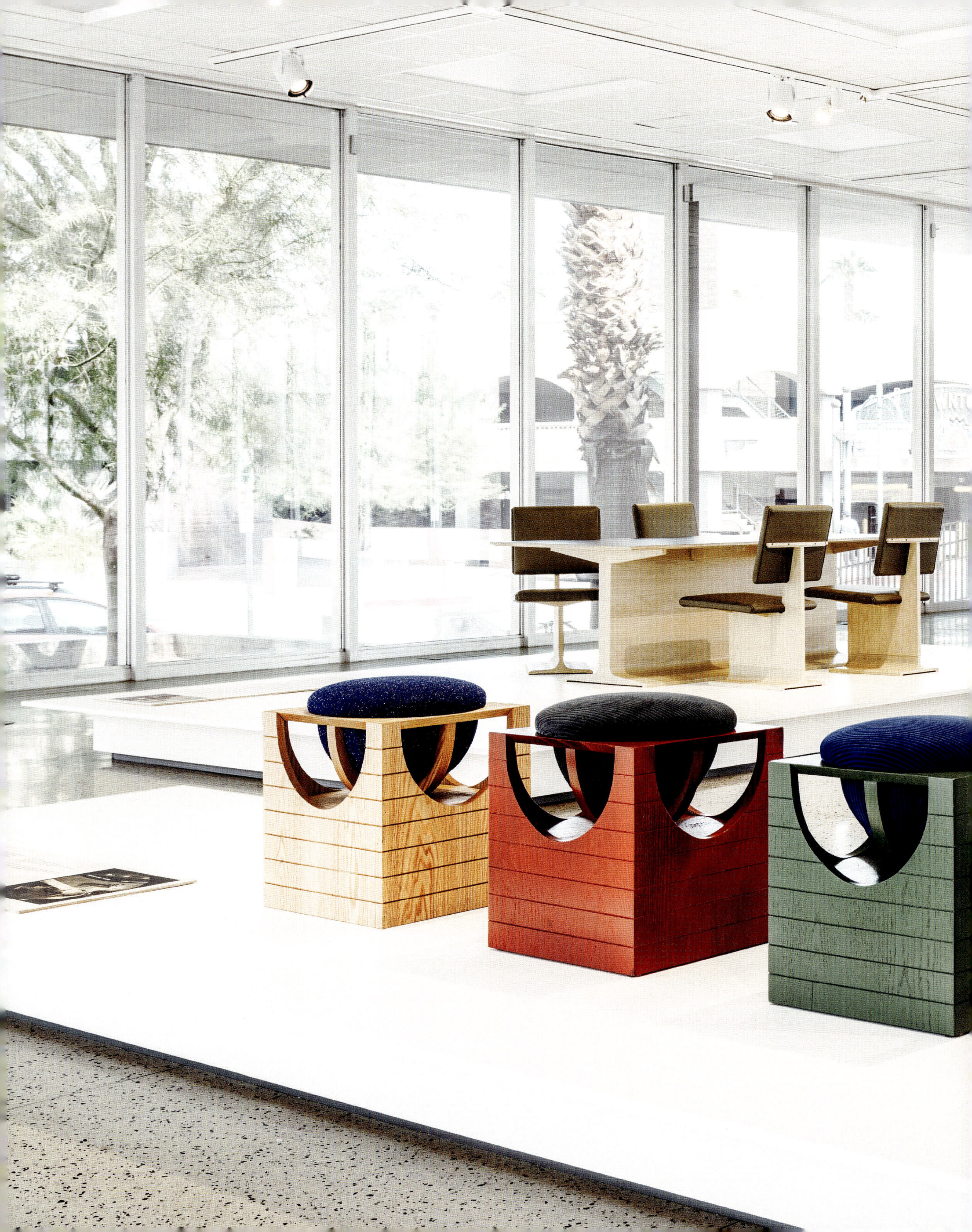

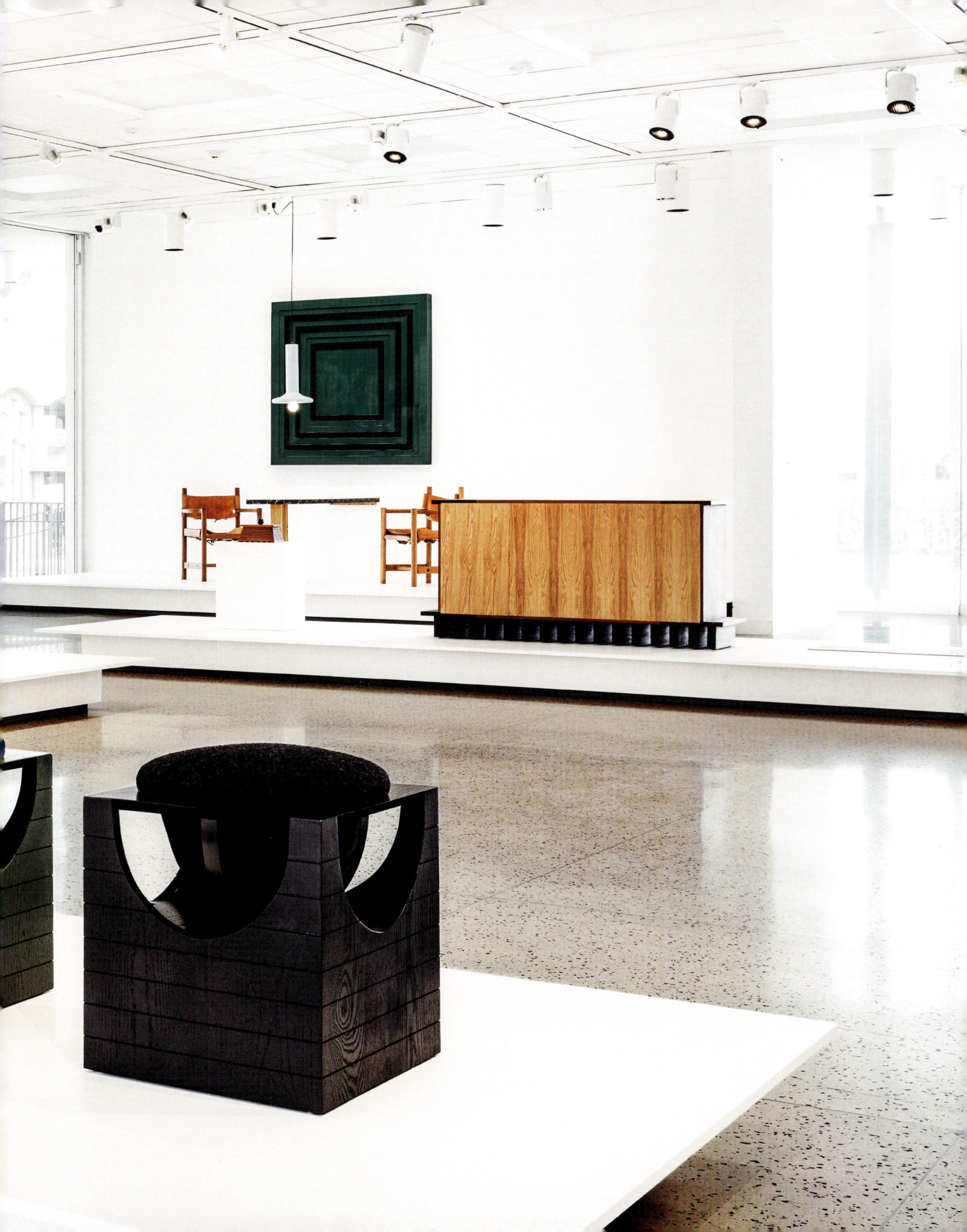

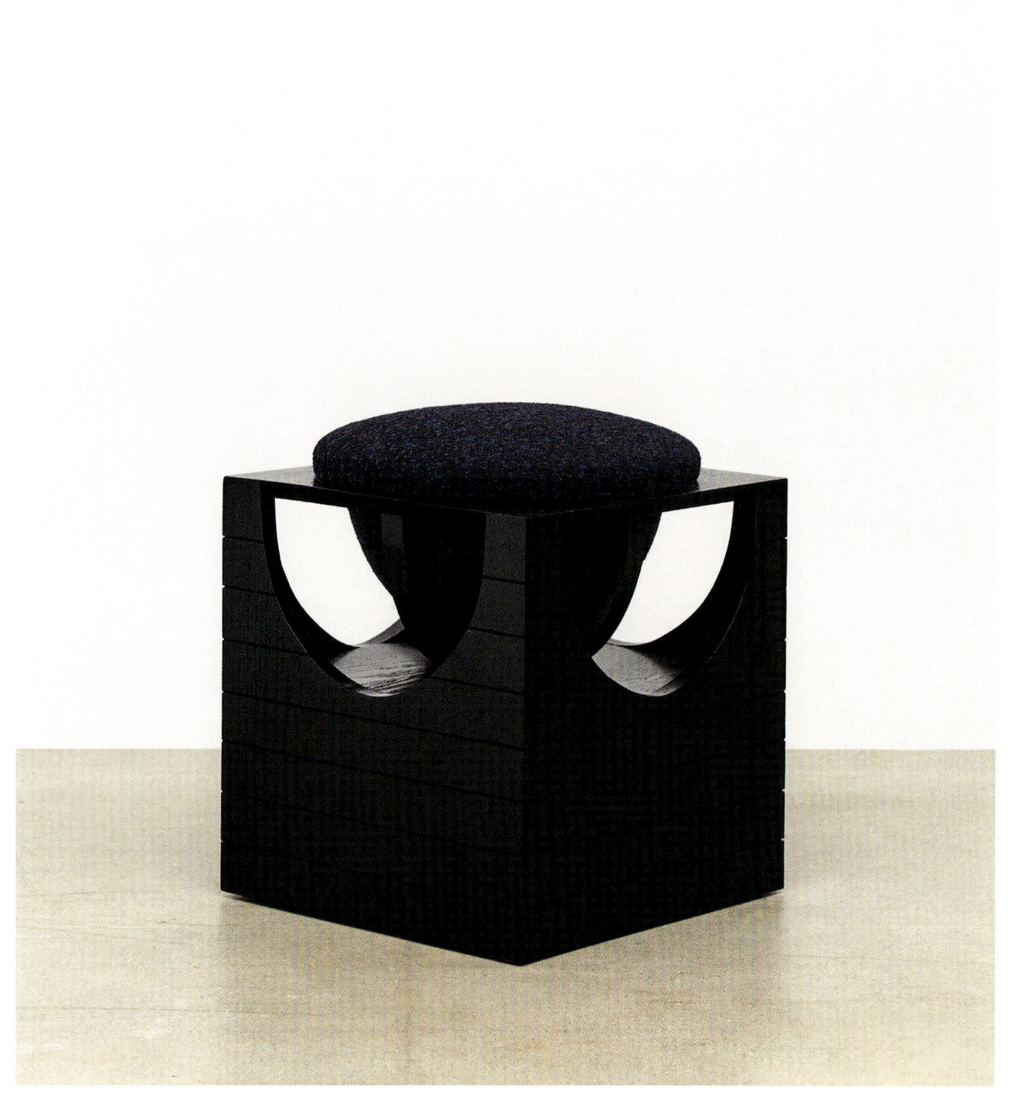

Sandoval Stool (Black), 2024
Lacquer on red oak and wool
19 × 16 × 16 in. (48.3 × 40.6 × 40.6 cm)

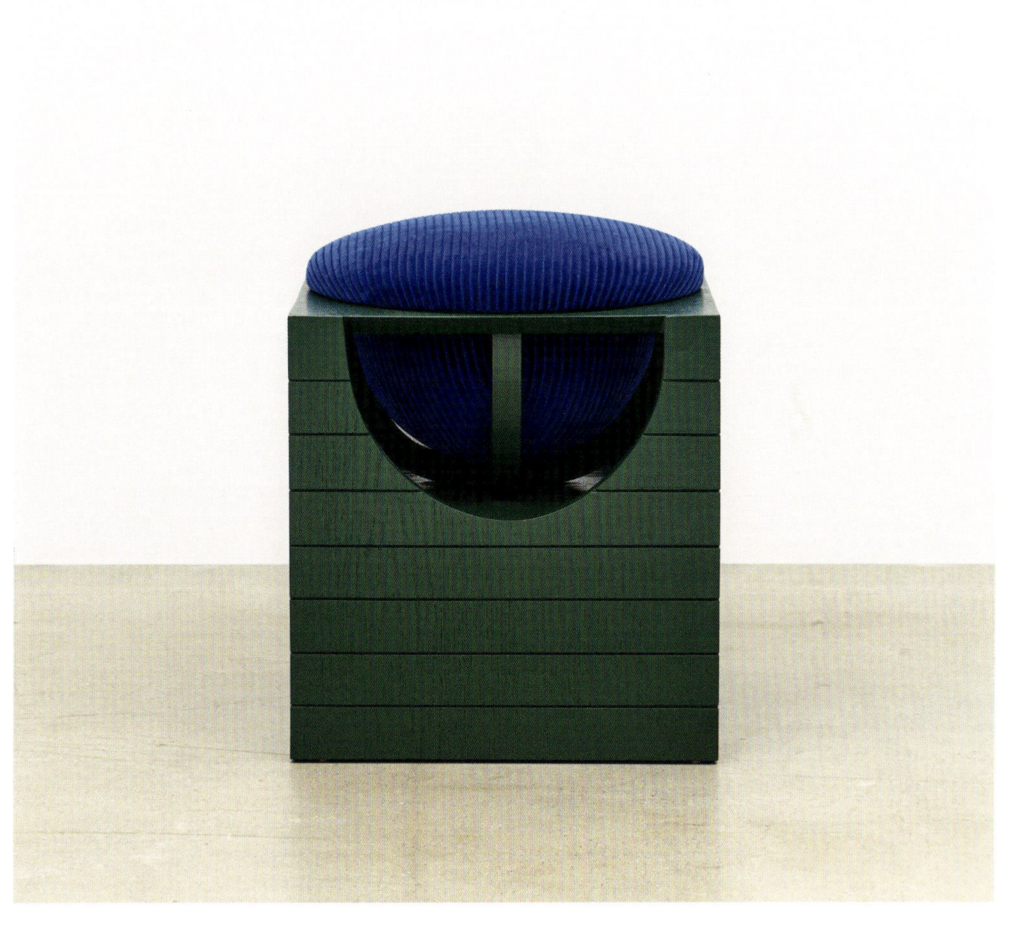

Sandoval Stool (Green), 2024
Lacquer on red oak and wool
19 × 16 × 16 in. (48.3 × 40.6 × 40.6 cm)

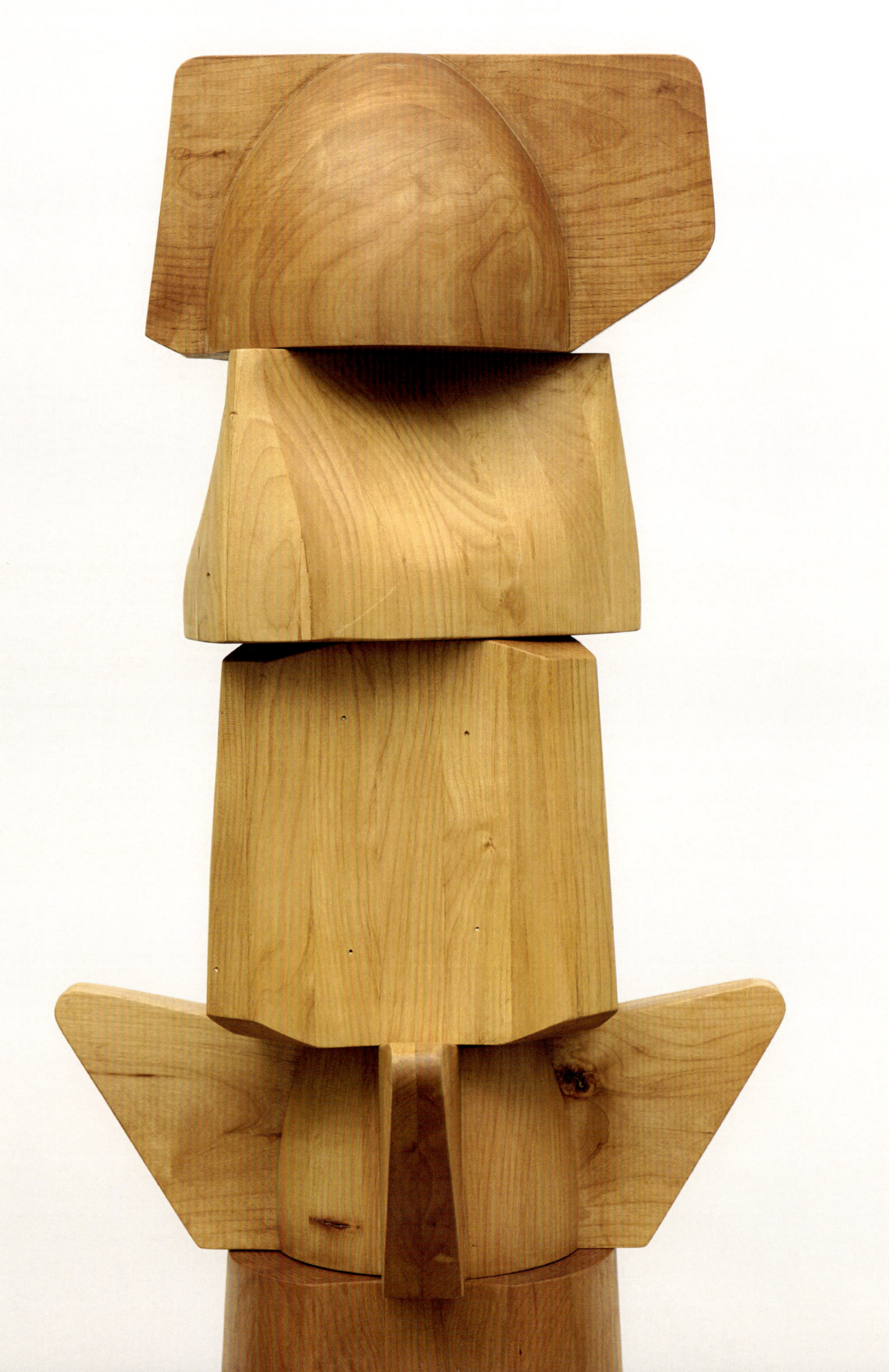

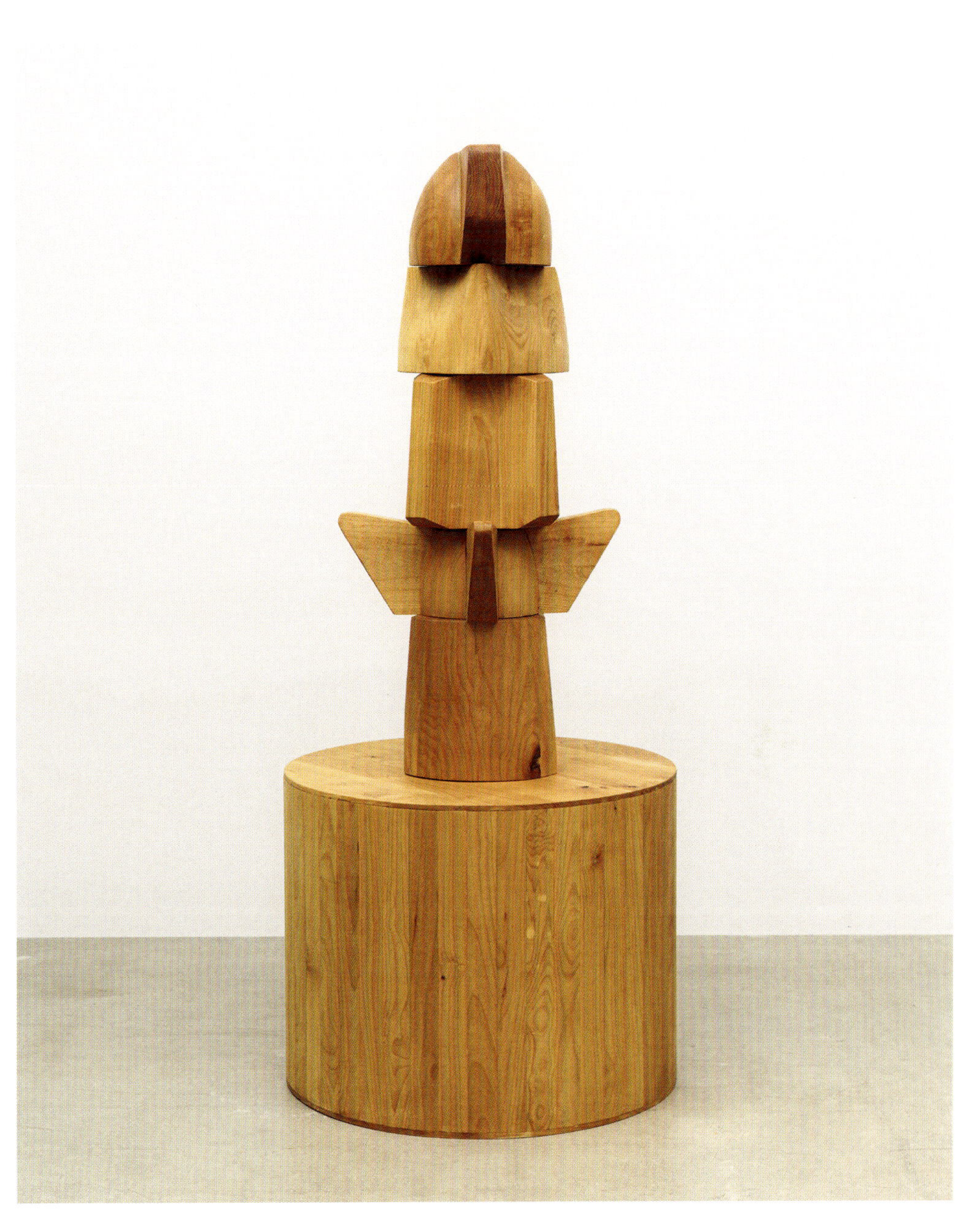

Totem (Gentle on My Mind), 2024
Alder
71⅞ × 30 × 30 in. (182.6 × 76.2 × 76.2 cm)

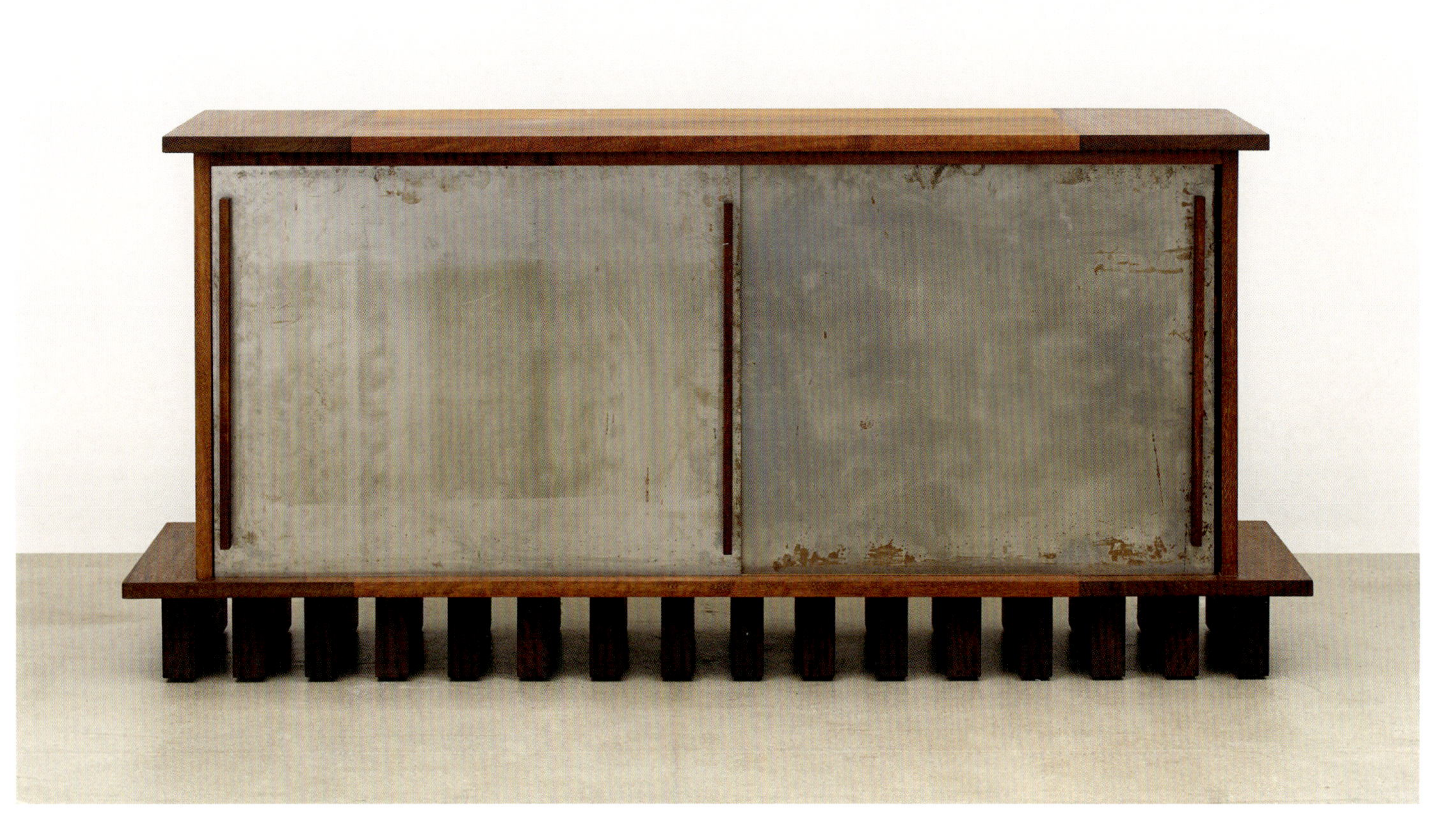

Sixteen, 2022
Ipe and steel
31⅜ × 67 × 17 in. (79.7 × 170.2 × 43.2 cm)

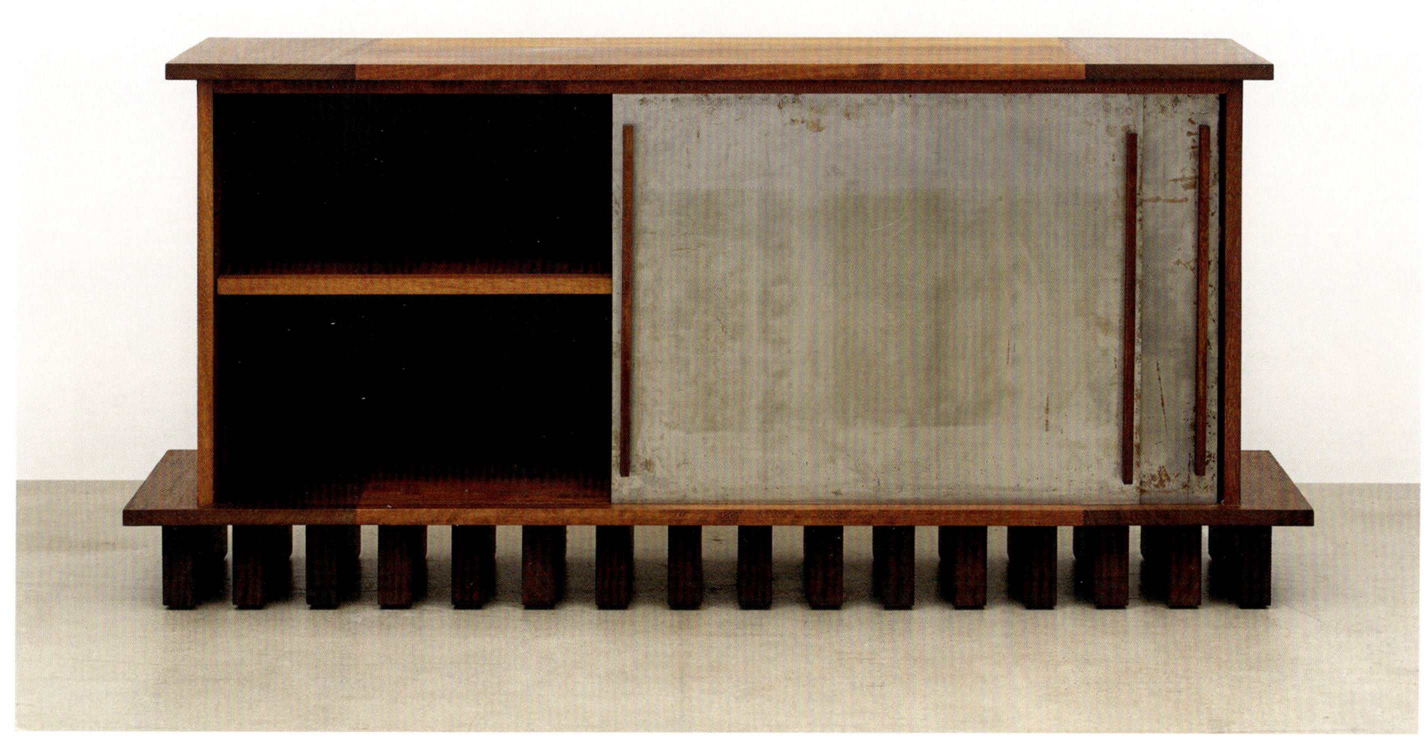

Hanging Out, 2024
Lacquer on red oak
20 × 14 in. (50.8 × 35.6 cm)

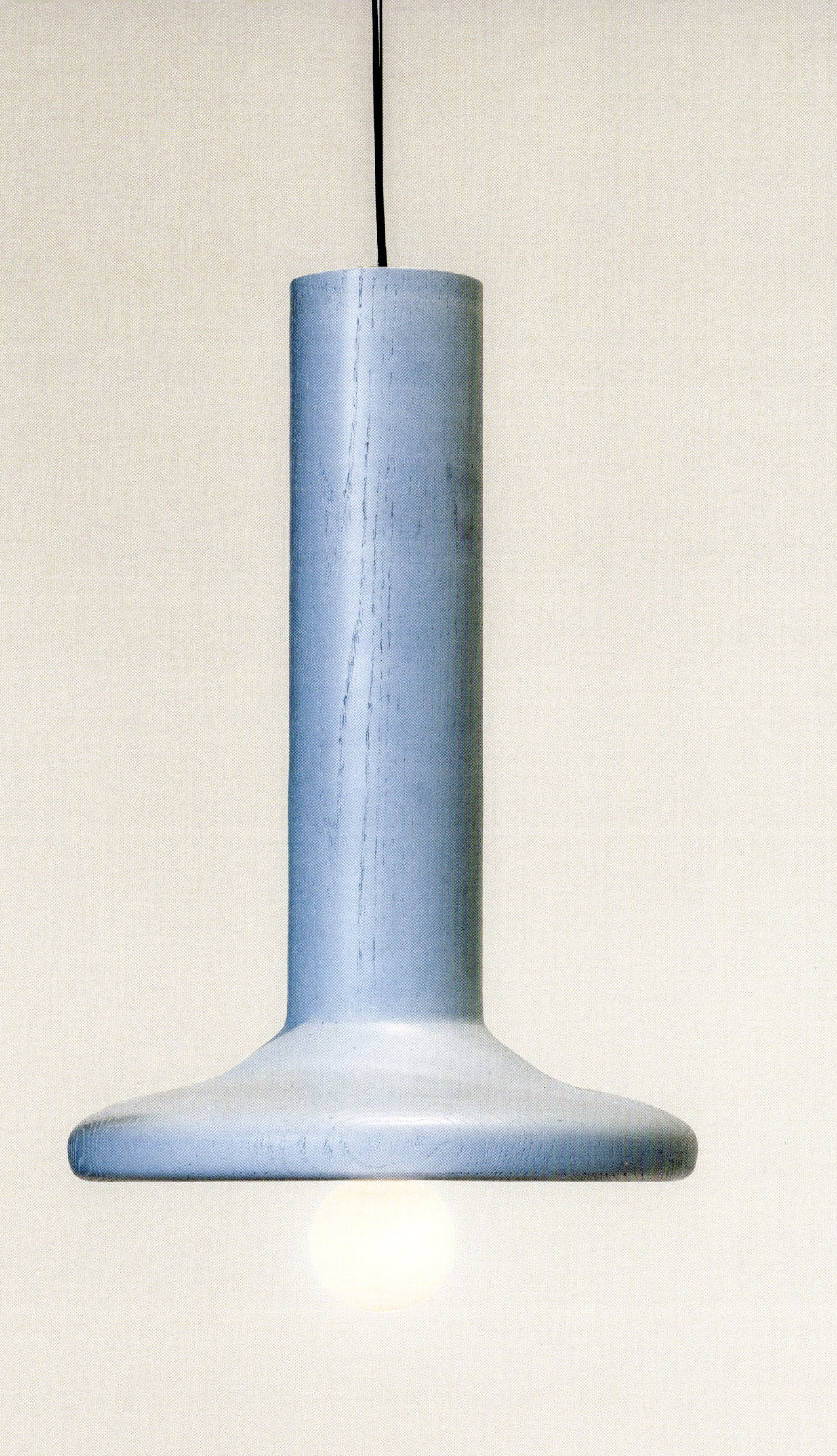

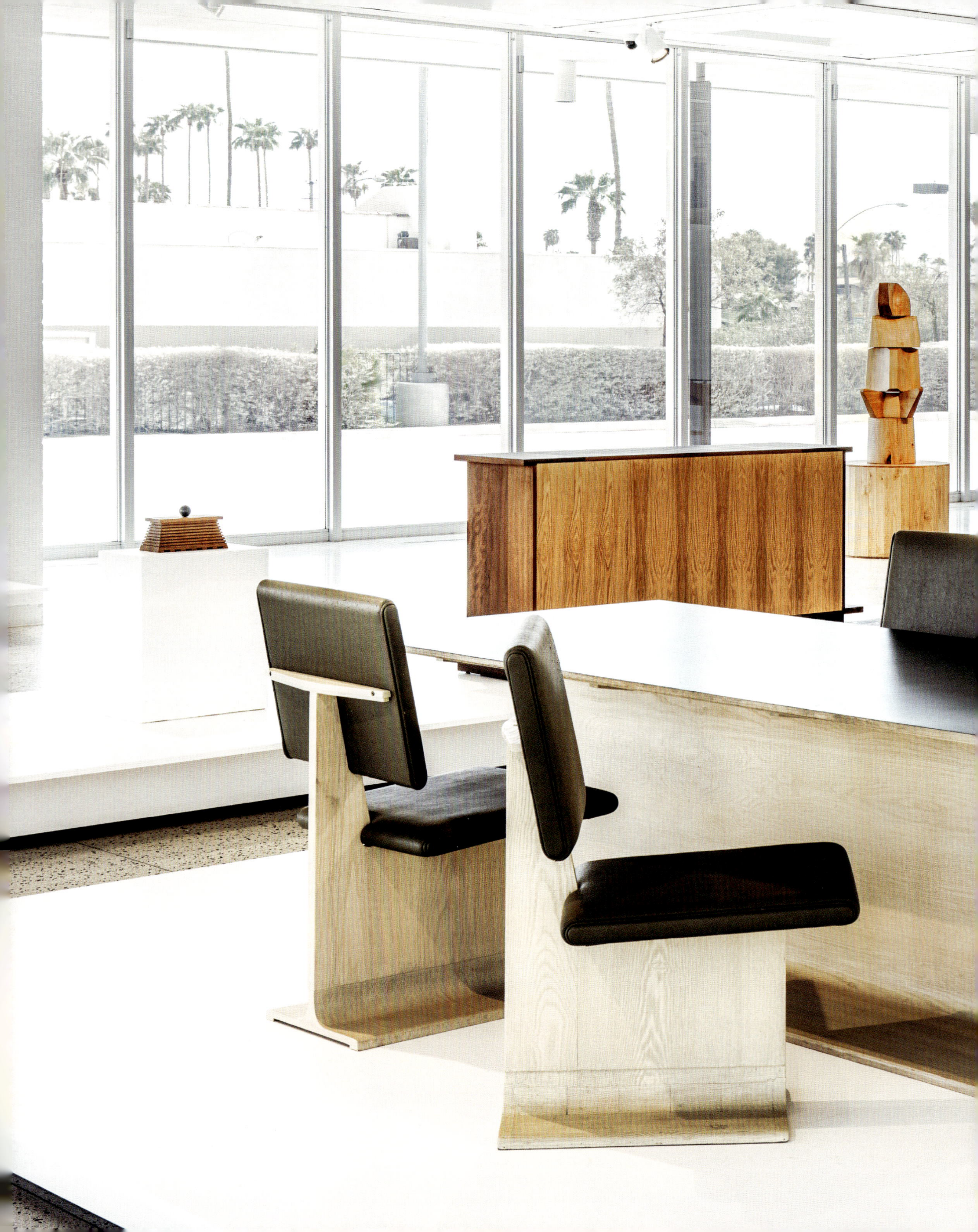

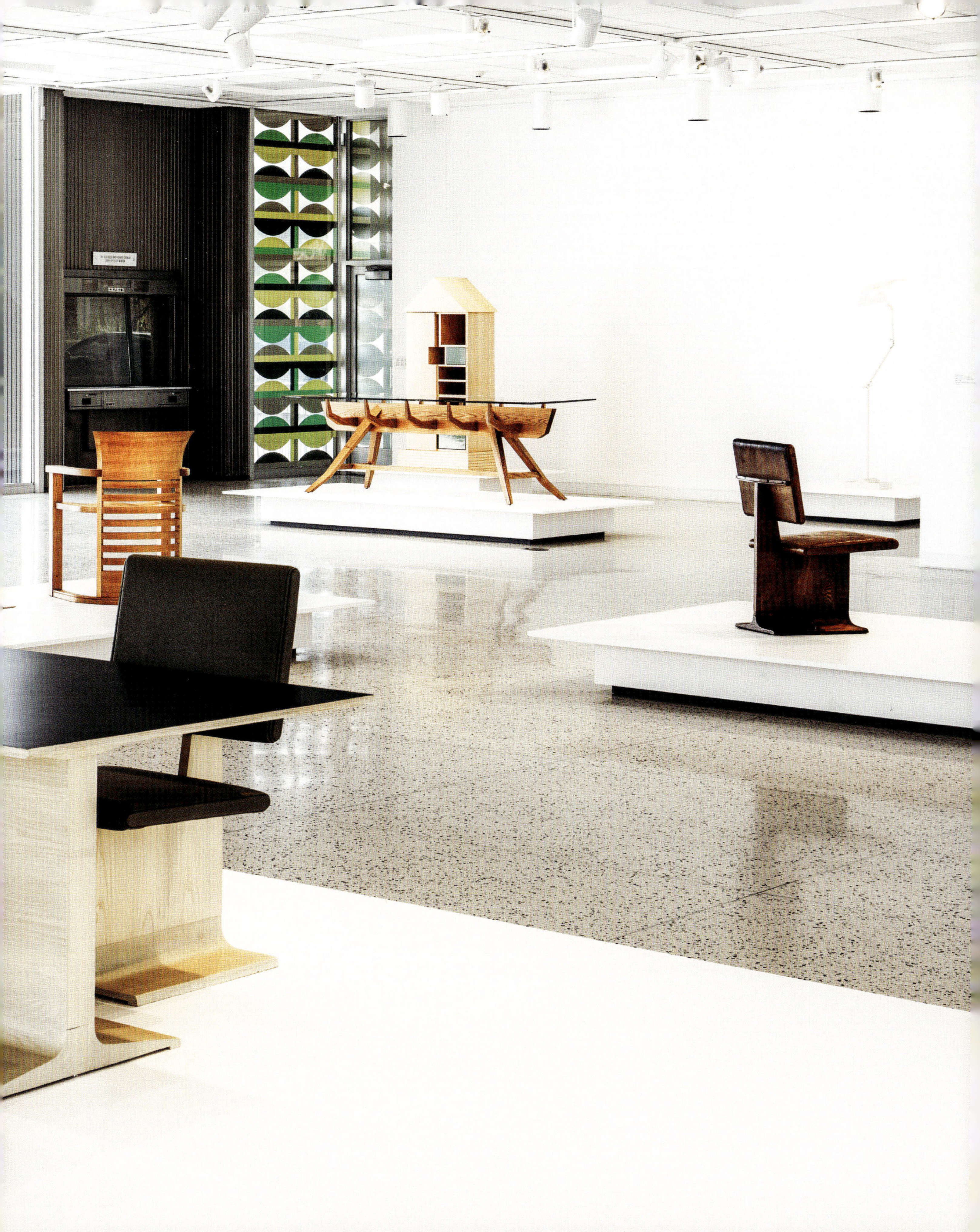

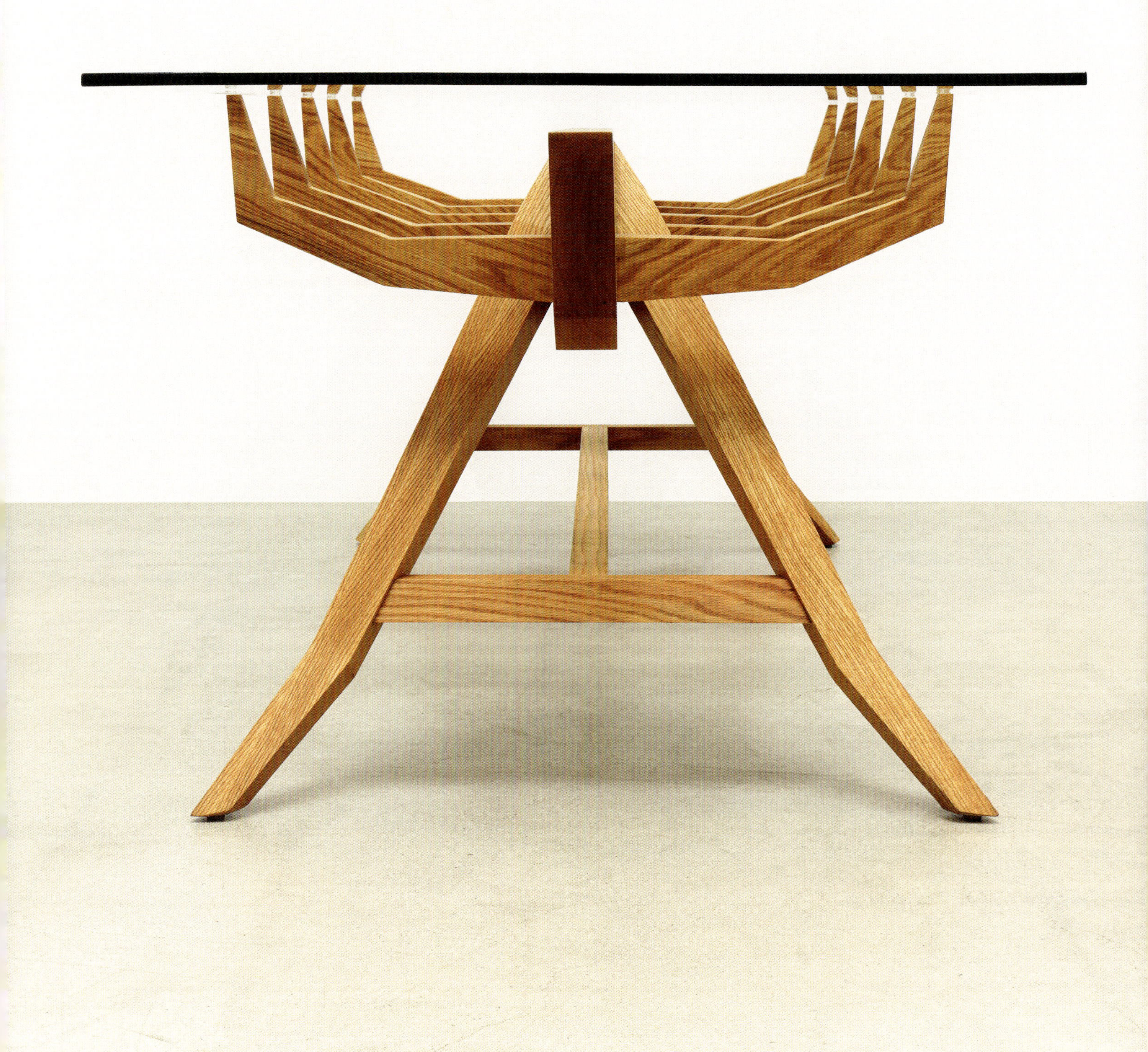

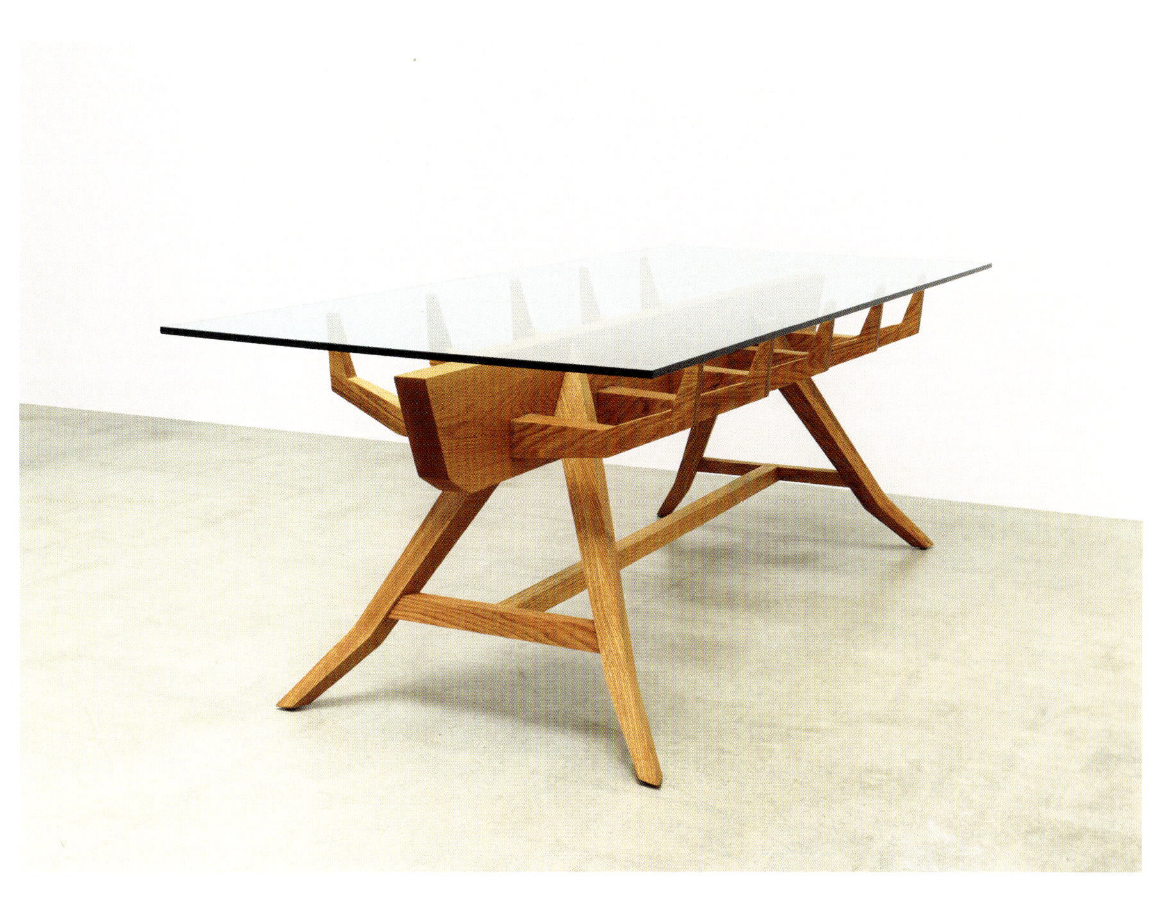

Toro table, 2023
Red oak and tempered glass
29¼ × 84 × 36 in. (74.3 × 213.4 × 91.4 cm)

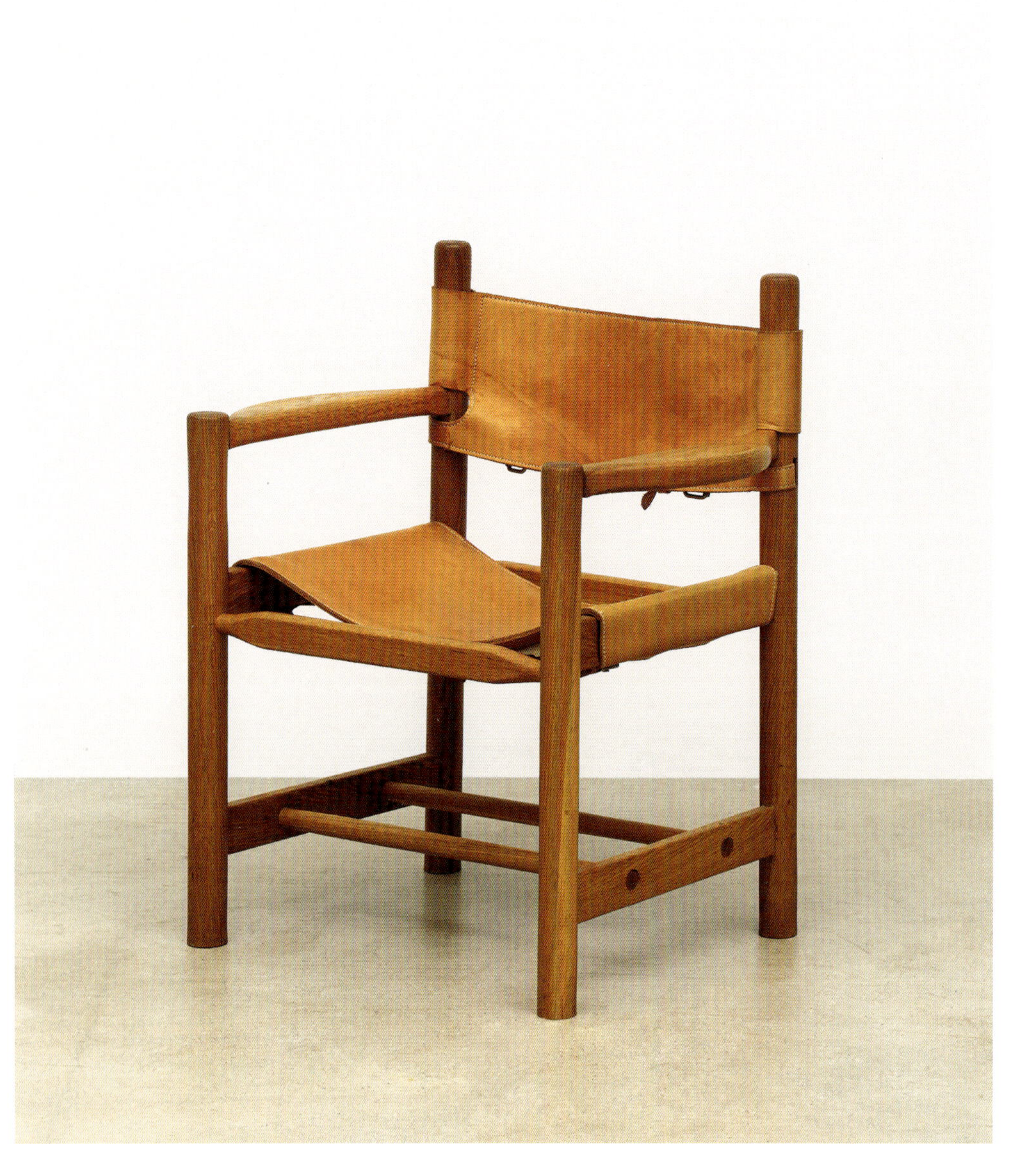

Chumash Chair, 2019
Red oak and leather
33 × 28 × 18½ in. (83.8 × 71.1 × 47 cm)

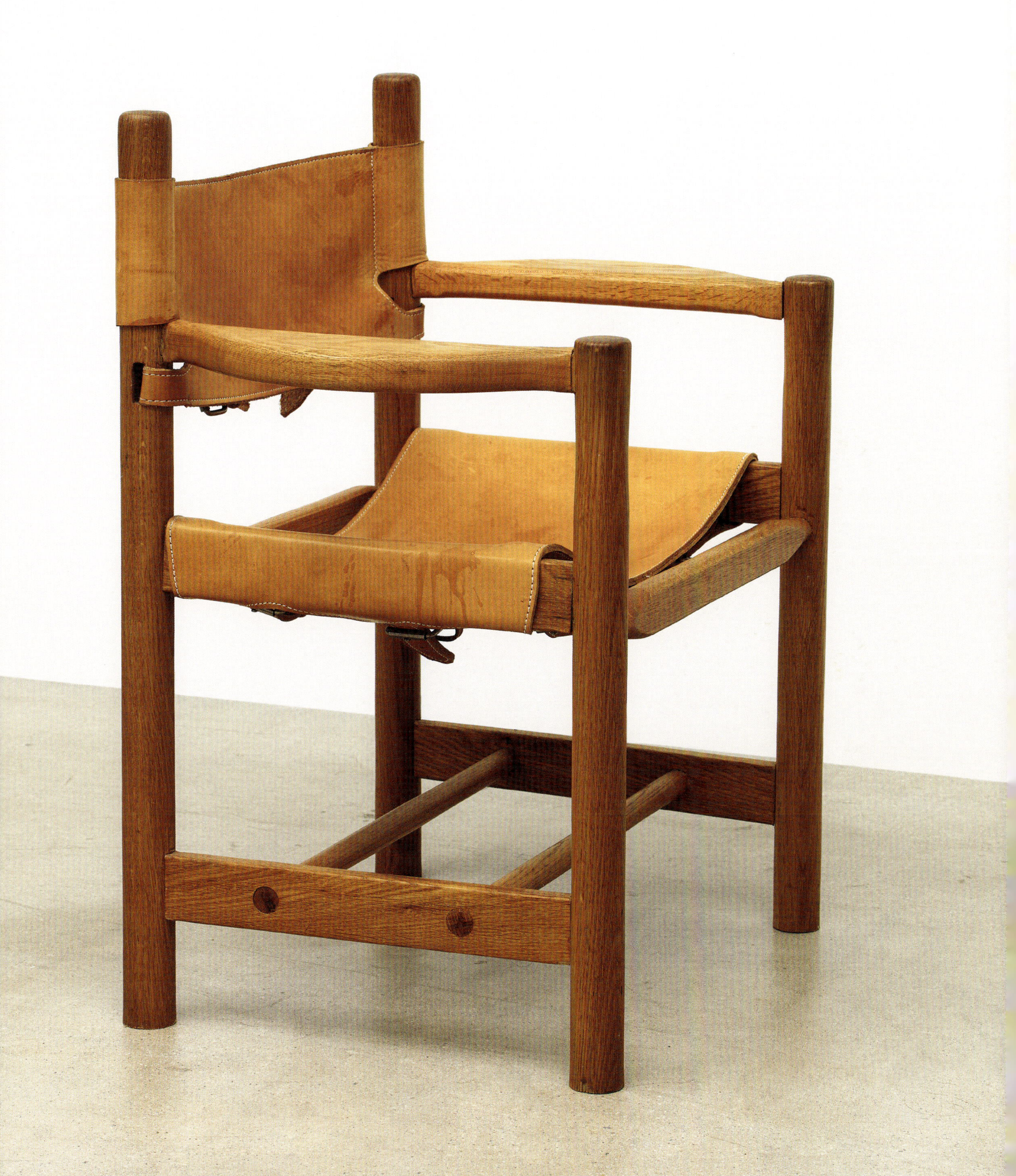

Sandoval Stool (Red), 2024
Lacquer on red oak and fabric
19 × 16 × 16 in. (48.3 × 40.6 × 40.6 cm)

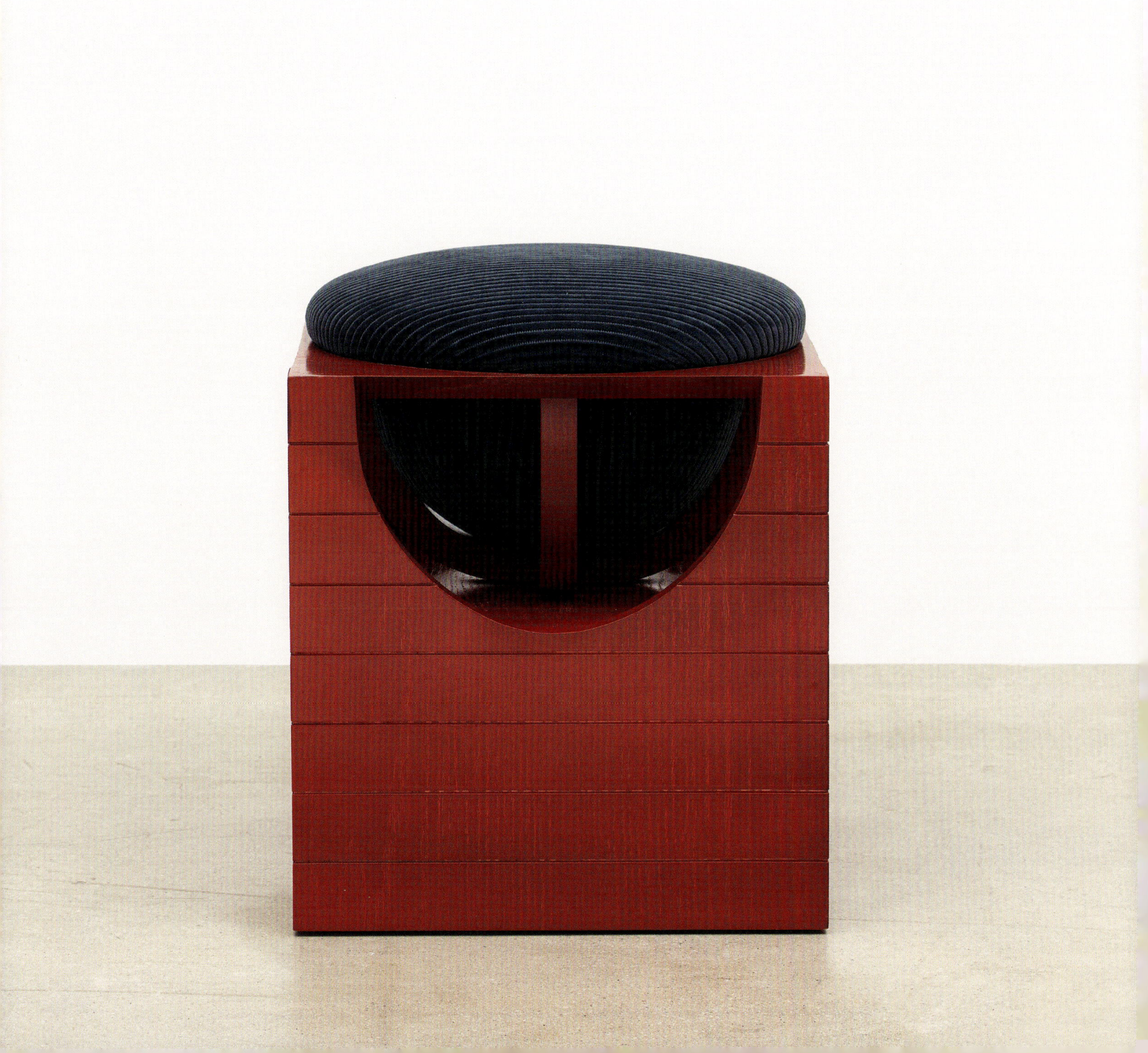

This book is published in conjunction with

So Near, So Far
Ryan Preciado—Manuel Sandoval

Palm Springs Art Museum
Architecture and Design Center
Edwards Harris Pavilion
300 South Palm Canyon Drive
October 5, 2024–April 13, 2025

Edition of 750

Design and production: Mei Lenehan, Karma Books
Editor: Sophia Larigakis, Karma Books

Printed and bound in Italy by Faenza Printing Spa

Page 7, left: courtesy R. M. Schindler papers, Architecture and Design Collection. Art, Design & Architecture Museum, University of California, Santa Barbara; page 7, right, photo: Lance Gerber; pages 9, bottom, and 27 © J. Paul Getty Trust. Getty Research Institute, Los Angeles. Photos: Julius Shulman; page 10, photo: Carlos Jaramillo; pages 13, 14, 19, and 20: © 2024 Frank Lloyd Wright Foundation. Courtesy the Frank Lloyd Wright Foundation Archives at the Museum of Modern Art | Avery Architectural & Fine Arts Library, Columbia University, New York. Licensed by Artists Rights Society; page 16, top: courtesy Wisconsin Historical Society. Photos: Angus Vicar; page 16, bottom: © 2024 Frank Lloyd Wright Foundation. Licensed by Artists Rights Society. Courtesy the Frank Lloyd Wright Foundation Archives, New York. Digital Image © The Museum of Modern Art/Licensed by SCALA / Art Resource, New York; page 21 © 2024 Frank Lloyd Wright Foundation. Licensed by Artists Rights Society / Victoria and Albert Museum, London; page 24, photo courtesy of Clars Auctions; page 26, courtesy Library of Congress

Pages 42–43, 50–51, and 60–61: *So Near, So Far: Ryan Preciado—Manuel Sandoval*, installation views, Palm Springs Art Museum, October 5, 2024–May 12, 2025. Photos: Lance Gerber

ISBN: 978-1-961883-22-2